MW01258152

ALLAH WEEPS

A Christian Perspective
of Modern Radical Islam

ALLAH
WEEPS

A Christian Perspective
of Modern Radical Islam

S. F. FLEMING

© 2017 by Selah Publishing Group, Bristol, TN. All rights reserved

Printed in the United States of America

All scripture quotations are taken from the New King James Version, Thomas Nelson Publishers, Nashville: Thomas Nelson Publishers, © 1982. Used with permission. All rights reserved.

No part of this book may be reproduced, stored in a retrieval system, or transmitted in any way or by any means—electronic, mechanical, photocopy, recording, or otherwise—without prior permission by the copyright holder, except as permitted by USA copyright law.

ISBN 978-1-58930-302-7

Library of Congress Control Number: 2017934439

Acknowledgments

I would like to thank Garlen Jackson and Selah Publishing Group for asking me to write my original manuscript on Islam in 2002. It was that impetus that ignited a greater desire on my part to learn about the subject. Now, again, all of these years later, it is Selah Publishing Group that is helping with the publication of this current book. Thank you so much!

To my daughter, Susanna Fleming, who helped with some of the initial editing, I am very grateful. She did a masterful job. I appreciate the continued support of my wife, Kathleen, our family members, and my friends and colleagues who encourage me and pray for my ministry.

Many of the personal experiences recorded in this book that took place among Islamic people would not have been possible if not for the faithfulness of the supporters of Gate Breaker Ministries. It is because of the faithfulness of these individuals and churches that I can travel to various countries around the globe and impact the people there for Christ. God bless all of you!

Dedication

To Rizwan and Asher,

faithful ministers and partners

with Gate Breaker Ministries

in Pakistan since 2009

Translations

The word *Koran* means "to recite." It can be spelled in various ways: *Qur'an*, *Qor'an*, etc., but for the sake of consistency, this book uses the word *Koran*. All quotes from the Koran are taken from two different translations, for clarity. One was translated by J. M. Rodwell, and it uses more archaic English as compared to the more modern English version translated by M.A.S. Abdel Haleem.[1] The words that have been translated by Haleem will be noted. Please also note that if you compare the sura numbers (the word *sura* can mean either "chapter" or "verse") from two or more different Korans, the verses will vary somewhat, because the actual verse numbers have never been standardized.

---

[1] I will be using both *The Koran*, translated by J. M. Rodwell (Rutland, VT: Charles E. Tuttle Co., Inc., 1994), and *The Qur'an: A new translation* by M.A.S. Abdel Haleem (Oxford, England: Oxford University Press, 2010), in this book.

Contents

Foreword

Over the past two decades, events in the United States and the Middle East have thrust the religion of Islam into the forefront of conversations around the globe. Experts have come out of the woodwork to explain to an incredulous world why a religion touted as a "way of peace" could endorse and even encourage the savage destruction of innocent human lives as a means of attaining Paradise for the suicidal perpetrators.

Even after years of public discussion, confusion still persists. Experts disagree on whether Islam condones or condemns jihadist violence. Perhaps the most simple explanation for the rise of Islamic militant behavior in recent years comes from the understanding that the word *Islam* doesn't actually mean "peace"—as many believe. It is more accurately translated as "submission."

Islam doesn't promote an ordinary submission. Rather, it demands submission to an unknowable god, who requires complete obedience without offering any individual follower the slightest luxury of discerning his will. So, the followers of Allah must turn to religious teachers, who function as ad-hoc interpreters of Allah's will.

Often, tremendous license is granted to Islamic teachers—without real accountability. Unscrupulous teachers can sometimes mix the words of Muhammad with the devotion of sincere Muslims in order to advance their own personal or political agendas. The results of this unscrupulous behavior can be disastrous, as can be seen from the rise of Boko Haram in Nigeria in recent years.

Having spent a number of years in Africa, I witnessed the extreme discomfort of Muslims living in a society where the teachings of Islam and the Gospel of Christ were presented side by side. It was inconceivable to Islamic leaders that individuals should be given the option of choosing between Islam and Christianity. Yet the Gospel resonates with many Muslims who earnestly desire a relationship with God, who is not distant and cold, as Allah seems to many of his followers.

Throughout my experience of planting churches in northern Nigeria, the power of the Gospel allowed me to introduce people to the true God, who desires to be known. and it often overcame the fear that was motivating their devotion to the unknowable Allah. In other words, many Muslims will come to Christ—if only they are allowed to hear His message.

Dr. Stanley Fleming's book serves as a powerful tool, providing the reader with an accurate understanding of Islamic teachings. By design, it motivates Christians to both pray and respond to the challenge of living for Christ in a changing world. The Church must understand and confront the diabolical religion of Islam, as it continues to be one of the fastest-growing religions, even in the United States and Europe.

My personal prayer is that through the reading of this book, 1) every reader will discern God's deepest desire, His love for all people, 2) the life-changing message of Jesus Christ will penetrate every corner of our world, and 3) the reader will be convinced of God's relentless desire to seek and to save those who are lost.

—DR. BILL HENNESSY
Director of Evangelism
Network211
Springfield, Missouri, USA
May, 2016

PART ONE

ISLAM IN THE MODERN WORLD

—— ✡ ✝ ☾ ——

CHAPTER 1

New Realities

Mahomet established a religion by putting his enemies to death; Jesus Christ by commanding His followers to lay down their lives. [2] —

—Blaise Pascal

For Whom Has This Book Been Written?

Since America was attacked on September 11, 2001, the world has reeled from many, many wars and numerous Islamic terrorist attacks that have shaken modern civilization to its core. Like many others, I have mourned as Islamic jihadists have maimed and killed innocent civilians in the name of their prophet and their god, Allah. In my years of ministry experience, however, I have also had the privilege to travel to many Islamic areas of the world, to meet with ministers and missionaries who are literally laying down their lives in service to God, in order to see Muslim people make personal commitments to the Lord Jesus Christ, and to witness the compassion of Christ in action.

This book has been written for those who want to learn more about Islam in the modern world from a Christian perspective. It has been written for Christians, Muslims, or any others who are searching for answers and who are open to consider the Christian perspective on the topic. There are many good secular books about

---

2 Blaise Pascal, *Thoughts on Religion and Philosophy* (W. Collins, 1838), Ch. XVI, p. 202.

Islam, but they do not always recognize the spiritual power of the Gospel message, the spiritual battle in which we are engaged, or that supernatural miracles, conversion experiences, Kingdom expansion exist, and they completely ignore the missional responsibilities of the Church.

Along with these challenges, it is vitally important for Christians to understand crucial issues facing Islam today. We will investigate both the modern and historical elements of Islam, as well as the Koran, the pillars of the Islamic faith, and its primary doctrines. What is it that has helped to grow and sustain Islam in the world? Why does it seem so formidable? What exactly is Islamic fundamentalism, and why does it attract so many Muslims? At what rate is Islam growing in our world today? What is the commitment level of the average Muslim? Is the religion of Islam losing adherents? In what ways can Christians reach out to Muslims with prayer, love, and the witness of the Gospel? How does the Bible tell Christians to respond to people of other faiths, and why are so many Muslims beginning to experience dreams and visions of the Lord Jesus Christ in these modern times?

A Brief Portrait of Modern Islam

The religion of Islam was formed by Muhammad in the seventh century when he lived in the Arabian Peninsula, and it has since grown to become the second largest religion in the world—second only to Christianity. At the heart of the Islamic teachings is the Koran, which supposedly contains revelations from God himself to the man, Muhammad.

Moderate Muslims interpret the teachings of Muhammad as meaning to live in peace with everyone, but jihadist Muslims interpret the teachings of Muhammad quite differently: They believe that Islam should be spread through violence and war. This jihadist worldview was birthed through the fundamentalist teachings of some Muslim clerics.

Of the approximate 1.7 billion Muslims in the world today, most just want to live their lives in peace.[3] They want to get a good education, raise their families, find good jobs, make significant contributions to society, and live with their neighbors in a civilized manner. I have met this very type of people throughout the world: in Palestine, Jordan, the United Arab Emirates, Pakistan, Indonesia, Malaysia, and elsewhere. *However*, there are also fundamentalist Muslims out there who do make up a minor percentage of Islam, and despite their smaller numbers, they should not be underestimated for the havoc they can unleash.

Controversy constantly broils over how many Muslims worldwide have been "radicalized." Some say the number is as high as 15 to 25 percent; others debate that the percent is much lower, maybe even only 1 percent.[4] In a 2013 survey by the Pew Research Center, 26 percent of Muslims in the Middle East had a favorable view of Hezbollah, and 25 percent had a favorable view of Hamas—and only 13 percent had a favorable view of the Taliban and Al Qaeda. Yet in the countries of Egypt, Malaysia, Lebanon, and the Palestinian territories, at least a quarter of the Muslim population who were surveyed *supported suicide bombings* in some instances if it was done to protect Islam and Muslim society.[5] The unfortunate reality today is that tens of millions of Muslims all over the world do sympathize with various aspects of what these Islamic terrorist groups are doing.[6] And now, through the adherents to jihadist principles, the world has now witnessed decades of Islamic terrorist attacks and wars.

The two main sects of Islam include the Shia and the Sunni. They differ in their concept of religious authority, theology, religious practices, and a strict or loose interpretation of the Koran. The vast majority of Muslims in the world today are Sunni, between 80 to

3 "Christianity 2015: Religious Diversity and Personal Contact," in *International Bulletin on Missionary Research*, Vol. 39, No 1 (January 2015): 29; gordonconwell.edu.
4 Alexander LaCasse, "How many Muslim extremists are there? Just the facts, please," *Christian Science Monitor* (January 13, 2015); csmonitor.com.
5 "Muslim Publics Share Concerns about Extremist Groups," PEW Research Center (September 10, 2013); www.pewglobal.org.
6 Ben Shapiro, "The Myth of the Tiny Radical Muslim Minority," *Breitbart* (September 4, 2014); breitbart.com.

85% of them. The Shia minority accounts for just 15 to 20 percent, with large populations of Shia Muslims living in Iran, Iraq, Pakistan, and India.

Many aspects of Islam seem to have been carried down through the generations, straight from the seventh century, because that was the "perfect" era in which Muhammad and his religion could thrive. For instance, the plight of Muslim women today has become a significant issue. In some Islamic countries, women are forced to wear burkas out of fear and to avoid beatings, arrest, or even honor killings. In thirty countries in Africa, Asia, and the Middle East, women still must suffer from female circumcision.[7]

Of the fifty-seven nations that belong to the OIC (the Organization of Islamic Cooperation), the average literacy rate among women in their populations is only 64 percent.[8] So, at least one-third of Muslim women are illiterate, and in many countries, the literacy rate is actually much lower.

Under Sharia law, a woman's testimony in court is worth only half that of a man's. A daughter's inheritance is only half that of her brother's. A wife cannot leave the country—or even her own house—without her husband's permission. If a woman is raped, there must be *four* witnesses to the crime; otherwise, the man usually goes free and unpunished.[9]

Regarding their adherence to the faith, individual Muslims can be quite devoted to Islam. Muslims are required to pray five times each day, attend a local mosque on Fridays, memorize large portions of the Koran, fast for the month of Ramadan each year, travel to visit Mecca once in their lifetimes, and also give to the poor. The vast majority of Muslims subscribe to these basic tenets of Islam.

However, as with any religion in this world, those who associate with Islam vary greatly in their level of devotion, as well as

---

7 Vanja Berggren, "Female Genital Mutilation: Studies on primary and repeat female genital cutting," (Stockholm: Karolinska University Press, 2005), 2–4.

8 "Education and Scientific Development in the OIC Member Countries," *Statistical, Economic, and Social Research and Training Centre for Islamic Countries*, SESRIC (2013), p. 6.

9 Michelle A. Vu, "Interview: Ex–Muslim Women on Life under Sharia Law," *Christian Post* (April 9, 2009); christianpost.com.

their method through which they demonstrate that devotion. For example, prayer is something that any Muslim can do, regardless of their socioeconomic status or their location, but the actual practice of it shows both the conformity and the diversity of adherents. One's commitment to pray five times per day—at daybreak, at noon, in the midafternoon, at sunset, and in the evening—is influenced by region and country. For instance, in the Islamic communities found in sub-Saharan Africa—such as Ghana, Cameroon, Nigeria, and Senegal—nine out of ten Muslims are committed to praying five times per day. However, in countries like Ethiopia, the DR Congo, Tanzania, and Mozambique, the numbers fall to only four to six out of ten. Conversely, in the regions of southeastern Europe and central Asia, the norm is only four out of ten or less. And in the countries of Albania and Kazakhstan, fewer than one in ten Muslims pray five times or more each day.

Making the once-in-a-lifetime pilgrimage to Mecca is rare for many adherents from any nation or region of the world, with the highest being only 17 percent from the Middle East–North Africa region. It would appear that the majority of Muslims observe the command to fast during the month of Ramadan, with lower numbers being reported in central Asia and southeastern Europe, and a similar pattern follows with giving alms to the poor.

Mosque attendance in central Asia and southeastern Europe is also low. Three out of ten Muslims in Russia never attend a mosque, nor do they read the Koran. In Uzbekistan, only three out of ten ever attend the mosque at all, but about half of them do read the Koran—at least sometimes. There are also the gender differences discovered regarding mosque attendance. The culture of a nation seems to influence this. In Pakistan, almost every man visits the mosque regularly, but five out of ten women never attend. In Azerbaijan, on the other hand, approximately six out of ten men and women have never visited a mosque.[10] Strangely, in the extremely theocratic nation of Iran, there are reports that mosque attendance

10 "The World's Muslims: Unity and Diversity," chapter 2, by Pew Research Center (August 9, 2012); pewforum.org.

has been falling off rapidly, and it may even be at an all-time low. One Western reporter was turned away from entering the mosque at Tehran University on the first Friday of Ramadan (the Islamic month of fasting); he was told that "the turnout was too meager for the eyes of a Western journalist."[11]

Lingering Controversy about the Attack on 9/11

Ask any American who is old enough to remember that day, and they can tell you precisely where they were and what they were doing when they learned of the terrorist attacks in our country on September 11, 2001. On that day, shock set over the entire nation, due to what was the worst attack on American soil since the bombing of Pearl Harbor in WWII.

For the most part, America has moved on past the atrocity of September 11, 2001, when nineteen Al Qaeda terrorists hijacked four passenger airliners headed from the East Coast to California, and used the planes as weapons. Two of the planes crashed into the twin towers of the World Trade Center in New York City, one plane crashed into the Pentagon building in Arlington County, Virginia, and the fourth airliner was probably aimed at the Capitol Building or the White House in Washington D.C., but heroic passengers wrestled with the hijackers, and it ultimately crashed in a field just outside of Shanksville, Pennsylvania. Nearly three thousand people were killed that day, and ten billion dollars in property and infrastructure damage was created.

The nation rallied together the best that it could during that sad time, by sending aid and volunteers to help in the aftermath. People all over the nation stopped what they were doing and prayed. Policemen and firemen gave their lives to rescue victims who were trapped in the damaged and collapsed buildings. There are many, many heroic stories of people who sacrificed their own lives, and who gave of their time, money, and other resources to bring about restoration in the weeks and months following the event. Churches took up offerings to send to the families of the victims and to help

11 David Blair, "Friday prayers in the Islamic Republic of Iran—but where are the worshipers?" *The Telegraph* (August 1, 2015); telegraph.co.uk.

with the cleanup efforts. Law enforcement agencies quickly investigated, trying to track down anyone who had been involved in the attack. Within one month, the United States launched a war in retaliation against the Taliban in Afghanistan, primarily because of their refusal to hand over Osama bin Laden, the mastermind who had been behind the attacks on America on that dark day.

Yet, even after all of these years, there are still suspicions that some of the leaders in Saudi Arabia (America's supposed "ally") were responsible for funding the attack. Of the nineteen hijackers, fifteen had come from Saudi Arabia, and it would appear that at least two of them had settled in San Diego before the attacks and received financial assistance from the Saudis. The Saudi government has officially denied any role in the attack, however, and the 9/11 Commission of 2002 said that their investigators had found "no evidence that the Saudi government, as an institution, or any senior Saudi officials individually funded al Qaeda."[12] However, twenty-eight pages of the 9/11 Commission Report were withheld from the public—the pages that dealt with "foreign support for the September 11 hijackers." These twenty-eight pages were eventually "declassified" on July 15, 2016 and released to the public.

In response to the release of these pages, one reporter wrote, "While the report's newly released pages do not state conclusively that Saudi officials collaborated with the hijackers, it does cast suspicion on members of the Saudi government, including a member of the Saudi royal family, Prince Bandar bin Sultan."[13] Among the various connections that the report reveals between certain Saudi officials and the terrorists, it states that Prince Bandar, the Saudi ambassador to the United States, made payments to a supporter of Osama bin Laden. This supporter also bragged about helping two of the hijackers of Flight 77 attempt their mission. Also, an unlisted phone number linked to Bandar was discovered in a phonebook owned by an Al Qaeda operative in Pakistan. To see other

12 Paul Sperry, "How US covered up Saudi role in 9/11," *New York Post* (April 17, 2016); nypost.com.
13 Warren Mass, "Congress Releases Classified '28 Pages' of 9/11 Commission Report," *New American* (July 18, 2016); thenewamerican.com.

details of these declassified twenty-eight pages, they are currently available on Internet.[14]

The Growth Rate of Islam

In 1900, Islam made up 12 or 13 percent of the world's population, with approximately 220 million followers. Today, it accounts for roughly 22.5 percent of the world's population, at 1.7 billion individuals, with projections that this number will increase to 27 percent by the year 2050. Christianity has also continued to grow, continuing to be the largest religion in the world, with some 2.2 billion people following the Lord Jesus, but while Christianity has quadrupled in the last one hundred years, Islam has actually grown sevenfold. This is not because Muslims are evangelizing better than Christians, but because the rate of childbirth among Muslims in certain parts of the world (Egypt, Pakistan, Indonesia, and Bangladesh, for example) grew very high in the twentieth century, and these children have become Islam's newest adherents.

Though many Muslim nations have high birth rates, some, however, do not. Iran's rate of birth has plunged since the 1980s, as have Algeria's and Tunisia's, as well. Morocco and Turkey are also on a downward track. In his book *The Next Christendom: The Coming of Global Christianity*, author Philip Jenkins explains the potential disconnect that could occur in Islam as a result of these population differences:

> The Islamic world thus seems to be dividing into a two-tier model, a demographic schism between countries with low fertility rates, and those with rates at 5 or 6—countries such as Pakistan, Egypt, and Saudi Arabia. The highest birthrates of all are in such nightmare lands and failed or failing states as Iraq, Somalia, Sudan, Afghanistan, and Palestine/Gaza. Quite possibly, low-fertility countries will become more secular, more European, in fact, while large-family nations remain religious. Algeria might have far more in common culturally and socially with France

---

14 Brian McGlinchey, "Saudi Government Links to 9/11 Shouldn't Stay Secret," *28 Pages* (June 12, 2016); 28pages.org.

than with Egypt. In that case, concepts of Muslim identity would become ever more tenuous, and so would any prospects for a future clash of civilizations.[15]

Some population experts say that by the year 2050, there will be a change in religious majorities in various countries, as Islam gains more adherents. Of the countries that have Christian majorities, this margin will decline from 159 to 151, whereas countries that already have a majority of Muslims will see an increase from 49 to 51. Actually, with the exception of Buddhism, all of the major world religions are projected to increase by the year 2050.[16]

However, some of this information are simply best guesses made by statisticians. There are a number of sources that challenge the notion that Islam is the fastest-growing religion in the world. For instance, Muslims used to outnumber Christians in sub-Saharan Africa, but a study published by the Pew Forum in April 2010 found that Christians now outnumber Muslims there two to one.

A 2009 survey in the United States also found that there are fewer than 2.5 million Muslims living in the U.S., a figure much smaller than what had been advertised. After 9/11, for instance, I remember news correspondents reporting that there were at least fifteen million Muslims living in the United States at that time. In numerous radio interviews that I did, I tried to correct this exaggeration. Of the current population of Muslims in the United States today, roughly two-thirds (or, 1.65 million) are first-generation immigrants from other countries. Some say that less than 7 percent even attend mosque regularly. Also, a respected Pakistani-born American Muslim, Dr. Ilyas Ba-Yunus (1932–2007), conducted research on apostasy, and he estimated that 75 percent of new Muslim converts ultimately left the religion of Islam within a few years.[17]

---

15 Philip Jenkins, *The Next Christendom: The Coming of Global Christianity, Third Edition* (New York: Oxford University Press, 2011), pp. 203–207.
16 "The Future of World Religions: Population Growth Projections, 2010–2050," *Pew Research Center* (April 2, 2015); pewforum.org.
17 "Seventy-five percent of new U.S. Muslim converts leave within three years," *Muslim Statistics* (December 14, 2012), l; muslimstatistics.wordpress.com.

This sounds on par with many other places. In China, Europe, the United Kingdom, and Russia, the number of adherents to Islam has been inflated, and among those who do convert and are then reported as adherents, a large percentage leave the religion within a few years. One example of this has been exposed in Russia, where it was widely believed that there were at least twenty million Muslims living there, but actually there were only between seven to nine million. And of those, only *three thousand* were ethnic Russians who had converted to Islam in a fifteen-year period. Yet, during that same period, two million ethnic Muslims *became Orthodox Christians* in that same area. Twenty percent of the Tatars converted to Christianity.[18]

In 2007, I spoke with a Tatar Muslim woman who had recently given her life to Christ. After I finished teaching at a church in Ukraine on the topic of "Jesus in the Koran," I gave an altar call. She came forward and asked me to pray for her, because she felt that God was calling her to become a missionary to Saudi Arabia.

Hold On! Who Is Coming Back Again?

With the phenomenal increase of Islam (largely due to high fertility rates in certain areas of the world), and the globally expanding spirit of jihad, the evangelism for Christ that Christians continue to undertake seems a bit daunting. It may seem difficult to believe that world evangelism will ultimately be victorious for our Lord and King, but let us pause and remember the words of the Lord Jesus Himself given in His Great Commission before He ascended into heaven:

> All authority has been given to Me in heaven and on earth. Go therefore and make disciples of all the nations, baptizing them in the name of the Father and of the Son and of the Holy Spirit, teaching them to observe all things that I have commanded you;

18 "Fastest Growing Religion," *WikiIslam*. Wikiislam.net has reported on many sources such as the Pew Forum on Religion & Public Life, April 15, 2010; Patrick Goodenough—New Survey on Islam Calls into Question Population Figure Used by Obama—CNS News, October 9, 2009; "Twenty million Muslims in Russia and mass conversions of ethnic Russians are myths—expert—Interfax," April 10, 2007 (accessed April 23, 2016).d

and lo, I am with you always, even to the end of the age. —Matthew 28:18–20 NKJV

Do you know who it is whom the Muslims expect to come again on Judgment Day? I'll give you a hint: It is *not* Muhammad. *It is Jesus!* That's right: Most Muslims believe that Jesus will come back to the earth again.

I have stood many times on the Mount of Olives in Jerusalem, overlooking tens of thousands of the graves of Jews, Christians, and, yes, even some Muslims who believed that that is the place where the Lord Jesus Himself will return to judge the world, based on Joel 3:2. This place is called the Valley of Jehoshaphat. However, most Muslims believe that Jesus will return on the *eastern* side of Damascus. Of course, they are not taught that Jesus is the Son of God. Instead, they are taught that when He returns to the earth, He will personally confirm that all the teachings of Islam are correct.

Yet, it is important for Christians to know about this strong tradition, as well as what the Koran says about the miracles and the Person of Jesus, which will be discussed later in this book. The suras (verses) reveal a position of respect for Jesus that can be used by thoughtful Christians as a bridge, to help Muslims come to know the truth about Him. John 14:6 tells us: "Jesus said to him [Thomas], 'I am the way, the truth, and the life. No man comes to the Father except through Me.'"

Though the task of evangelizing the world can appear daunting at times, it is always important for Christians to remember that the Lord Jesus Christ has been given all authority in heaven and on earth. He is in charge! He understands our challenges, but He also sees the need for all human souls worldwide to hear the Gospel message (the Good News): that He died on the cross for the sins of all men, that He was buried, and that He rose from the dead (see 1 Corinthians 15:1–4). The Bible tells us, "For God so loved the world that He gave His only begotten Son, that whoever believes in Him should not perish but have everlasting life" (John 3:16 NKJV). Have you asked Jesus to be *your* Lord and Savior? He loves you and His greatest desire is for you to come to Him and be with Him forever.

Forty days after Jesus rose from the dead, He ascended into heaven and He now sits at the right hand of the Father, but someday He will come back to earth again for all of those who put their trust and faith in Him. As the apostle Paul wrote, Christians look "for the blessed hope and glorious appearing of our great God and Savior Jesus Christ, who gave Himself for us, that He might redeem us from every lawless deed and purify for Himself His own special people, zealous for good works" (Titus 2:13–14 NKJV).

An Invitation to Pakistan

In 2007, after many years as a Christian educator and a lead pastor in Idaho, the Lord led me to step away from leading a church to begin a nonprofit organization called Gate Breaker Ministries (GBM). It was focused on Bible teaching, apologetics, short-term missions, and leadership development. Yet the Lord wanted to add to these goals the role of *compassionate ministries*, and He was about to take me on a spiritual journey to accomplish His plan in this area.

At the beginning of 2008, I received an e-mail from a youth pastor named Asher Aziz, who lived in Lahore, Pakistan. He was inviting me to teach in his church and his community. He said that they needed my ministry. When I told my wife, Kathleen, about his offer, we agreed that neither of us could imagine me going to Pakistan—and so I regretfully explained this to Asher. Not only were there Taliban forces in Pakistan who hated Americans, but there were also wars going on in nearby Iraq and Afghanistan. Moreover, how could I even know whether or not this was some type of clever deception and strategic lure to take me captive or even kill me? I had been trying to squelch a certain habit of mine—of being too trusting and believing the best about people and personalities on the Internet, only to find out later that sometimes people are frauds. But Asher asked me to pray about it and he said that he would have his church pray that I would hear from the Lord about his request.

Throughout the year, Asher occasionally contacted me, asking whether -the Lord had spoken to me yet. To be honest, I had not really prayed about it much (although I had told him that I would), because I knew that I was not going to Pakistan and I didn't know this guy at all—he was a perfect stranger to me. Besides that, I was busy. Toward the end of the year, Asher asked me again, and I gave him my same standard response: that the Lord had not spoken to me yet. A week later, around Christmastime, another youth pastor named Rizwan Fazal, from the same community, e-mailed me and asked me to come. I thought he was likely from the same ministry as Asher, so I e-mailed Rizwan back, told him that Asher had already written to me with the same request just the week before, and I asked him to please stop bothering me. When Rizwan responded to me asking who Asher was, I did not reply.

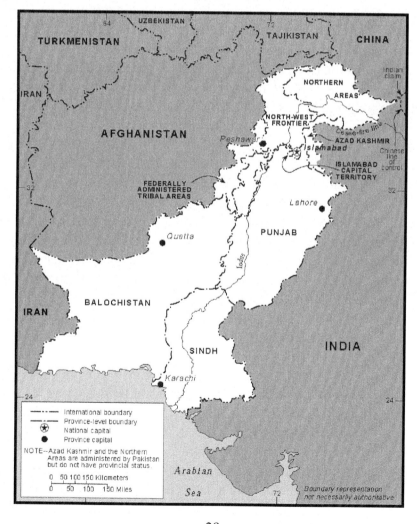

A few weeks later, on a Sunday afternoon in January 2009, I was sitting in Pastor Jess Slusher's living room in Quincy, Washington, after preaching that morning at Faith Community Church. After having taught his congregation a seminar on apologetics the day before, I was now alone, enjoying a football game on television. Suddenly, and as if out of nowhere, I felt a deep conviction settle in upon my spirit, and I heard the Holy Spirit speak, *Well, you said that you were going to pray about it—so, will you?* I immediately knew that this was in reference to the trip to Pakistan. I was shocked and awed, because I had not even remotely been thinking about it. So I turned off the television and I prayed quietly for about ten minutes. Basically, I asked the Lord to confirm whether or not He really wanted me to go, so that I would have no doubt about His will on this matter.

I finished the prayer and turned the television back on. The only people who knew about my invitation to Pakistan were my wife, the two youth pastors from Pakistan who had asked me to come, and me. I had not even told the board members of GBM—because I knew that I was not going to Pakistan! But within a minute of my turning the television back on, the pastor's wife, Lynn, walked from the kitchen and around the corner into the living room and she stood between me and the television, blocking my view. She proceeded to tell me that while she was in the kitchen, the Holy Spirit had given her a prophetic word for me. I was amazed at the timing and responded, "Okay." She told me then that it was only one word from the Spirit, but that I would know what it meant. Then she got close to me and shouted the word, "Go!"

I was astonished. "What did you say?"

Again, she shouted, "Go!"—and then she gave me $50 for wherever in the world that the Lord was sending me.

I pondered her words and actions all afternoon, praying for both clear direction and also about the topic that I was teaching at the church that night. The topic just happened to be "Answering Islam from a Christian Perspective." Right in the middle of my teaching that evening, however, the Holy Spirit told me to tell the congregation about the requests I had been given to go to Pakistan. So, I reluctantly told them about my invitation and about Lynn's word to me, but I also explained that the mission would be very expensive. I had looked up airfare by that point, and I mentioned how much it would cost. I did not ask the people for any money, but I did ask them to pray that I would know for certain the will of God in this matter. Pastor Jess then prayed for me. At the conclusion of that service, a couple in the congregation approached me to say that the Lord had asked them to provide me with a round-trip plane ticket to Pakistan. That was it—I knew I was supposed to go! Later that night, I called Kathleen and told her what had happened, and she simply said, "Well, I guess you are going to Pakistan."

That directive from the Holy Spirit took place over seven years ago. That May, I traveled to Lahore, Pakistan, for the very first time, and I met both Pastor Asher and Pastor Rizwan. In fact, they did not know each other; I introduced them. At that time, they were both single. Today, they are both married, have children, and are lead pastors. GBM has partnered with them to carry out significant ministry in the Punjab region of Pakistan. In 2014, Pakistan had a population of 184 million, making it the fifth most-populated country in the world, though physically, the landmass is roughly only twice the size of California. It is also the second-largest Islamic-dominated country. The city of Lahore, Pakistan, has a larger population than even New York City. According to the mission manual *Operation Mission*, the Punjab region of Pakistan "has a higher number of unreached individuals per Christian worker than any other place in the world."[19] The Christian population of Pakistan is about 1.5 percent. The need for Christian mission is great in that place!

Today, GBM has started two churches and has been involved in outreaches in which thousands of Muslims have made commitments for Jesus Christ. I have heard firsthand the stories from former Muslims who had dreams about Jesus, whom they did not even know, and the impact of the dream was so strong that it started them searching for this Man, which eventually led to their salvation. I have seen thousands of people stand up to make commitments to Christ, and I have prayed for Muslims who were seeking healing,

---

19 Jason Mandyrk, *Operation World: The Definitive Prayer Guide to Every Nation, Seventh Edition* (Colorado Springs, CO: Biblica Publishing, 2010), p. 664.

who received it from Christ, and who then gave their entire lives to Him. Praise the Lord for His faithfulness!

We have also added an entire dimension of compassion-based ministries to our portfolio these days. We started and we now maintain schools both for women and for indentured bond workers (that is, slave children). The GBM trade schools for women are two-year programs that train them to become seamstresses and/or beauticians. Though these programs were primarily started up with the purpose of empowering poor, disenfranchised, and underprivileged Christian women, we also let poor Muslim women attend. We provide sewing machines and teachers, and each day the women may take a break to pray to Jesus and to hear a reading from the Bible.

The GBM Hope schools were started for children who lived in and who had to labor in brickyard factories twelve hours per day/six days per week. These children are the poorest of the poor. There are thousands of brickyards in the Punjab area, and each one has bond workers, or as Pakistani pastors and residents call them, "slaves." These are people whose ancestors had borrowed money from the brickyards, but they could not pay it off, and so their children, grandchildren, great-grandchildren, and so on, are still there, getting further behind in debt each day and spending their entire lives making bricks. The government set a standard of working for children, that they may work no more than twelve hours per day and only six days per week, but they do not provide any education for these slave children. The government has basically turned a blind eye to this massive problem, because the making and selling of bricks is a significant portion of their annual gross national product. These types of bonded workers are labeled "slaves" by the United Nations, and it is estimated that 1.7 million children in Pakistan are such slaves. However, since there are no official statistics that can be taken, it is impossible to know for sure how many there actually are.[20]

---

20   Aliya Mirza, "2,000 minority girls converted to Islam forcibly: report," *Daily Times* (September 5, 2012); webcitation.org and Muslim Statistics/Slavery at wiki-islam.net.

One of the pastors whom I work with in Pakistan once told me that the government of Pakistan had recently made a change to help these children. International exposure to the brickyard slave problem caused the government to announce that the children would not be caused to owe the debt of their parents. Though that is a small step in the right direction, the problem remains. Children live in the brickyards with their parents, and they feel compelled to help their parents by making bricks to help pay off the debt. This, in turn, can trap them into a lifetime of being a slave. Also, the government has not been vigilant in following up with the brickyard owners, so a great amount of abuse still goes unreported. The government does not provide education for the children, and no education is free in Pakistan. Also, the slave children would have to find a way to travel to the schools in order to attend. So, the basic problem still remains.[21]

Our GBM Hope Schools offer free education, a few hours each day, five days per week, by certified teachers in rooms that are rented in the brickyards so that access for the slave children is easy for them. Because these schools were requested by Christian parents in the brickyards, the students will be taught various academic subjects like Urdu, English, mathematics, geography, science, and so on—but they will also be taught the Bible! For students who want to work to help their parents, they can go to school for a few hours and then still be able to work each day. The pastors in Pakistan think that the GBM Hope Schools will eventually lead these children into a future of hope and freedom. The children are being trained in skills that will empower them to one day get good jobs outside of the brickyards.

You can learn more about these GBM ministries by looking them up on YouTube, by searching for *Gate Breaker Ministries* on Facebook, or by visiting our website at www.gatebreakers.com.

Thank You, Lord Jesus, for providing direction to me and to the many others who follow You and desire to be a part of taking Your message of love and hope all over the world!

Rizwan Fazal, pastor and director of GBM Hope Schools in Pakistan. Interview by author, Lahore, Pakistan, October 21, 2016.

Later on in this book, we will consider some amazing stories of miracles of Muslims who have made decisions to follow Jesus after having had dreams of Him or having experienced other types of miraculous encounters. It is believed that there are more Muslims coming to know the Lord Jesus today than at any other time in history.

CHAPTER 2

Modern Islamic Fundamentalism

Individual Muslims may show splendid qualities, but the influence of the religion paralyses the social development of those who follow it. No stronger retrograde force exists in the world.[22]

—Winston Churchill

Salafi and the Muslim Brotherhood

The Islamic worldview is rooted in two things:

1. Muhammad, the seventh-century prophet of Islam
2. The Koran, a collection of revelations that Muhammad claims to have received from Allah

The rise of Islamic terrorists and their coalitions in modern times have brought Islamic fundamentalism to a new height in global affairs. This has resulted in great conflict within Islam. Two of the sources for the growth of this fundamentalism in the last century are the Salafi and the Muslim Brotherhood. Some consider both of these to be branches of Sunni Islam.

Salafism: The word *salaf* means "predecessors," and the basic idea behind this movement is that the first generations of Muslims, who conformed closely to Muhammad's model, are the best examples of how to live. Therefore, they believe, Muslims of today who desire to

22 Winston Churchill, *The River War, First Edition*, Vol. II (London: Longmans, Green, & Co., 1899), 248–50.

35

live in the "best way" will closely conform to the standards of living set forth by Muhammad and his immediate predecessors. Salafism is more of a worldview than an organization to which a person can belong. The idea stems from the sura (verse) below:

> The Messenger of God is an excellent model for those of you who put your hope in God and the Last Day and remember Him often.[23] (Sura 33:21, Haleem)

Salafism is a reform movement that strives to restore the purity of Islam. It embraces a strict adherence to jihad, to sharia law, and to separation from any modern Western ideals. *Wahhabism* is a form of Salafism, and it functions as the religious ideology of the state of Saudi Arabia. It is based on the fundamentalist teachings of an eighteenth-century teacher, Muhammad ibn Abd al-Wahhab.[24]

The Muslim Brotherhood: This organization, founded in Egypt in 1928 by its first and primary teacher, Hasan al-Banna, gained support from many Arabs who were dissatisfied with the results of the 1919 national revolution. The Muslim Brotherhood reacted negatively to the "British hegemony, and more generally against the modernization of the country on a Western model. In order to end the supremacy of European states over Arabs, the movement summoned its followers to jihad. Its main demand? Return their territory to that of an Islamic state and to a social order stringently oriented toward the Koran and Hadith.[25] Both of these are holy books to Islam.

Though the ultimate goal of both Salafism and the Muslim Brotherhood is to spread Islam to every corner of the world through jihad (and violence if necessary), one of the key differences today between the Salafi worldview and that of the Muslim Brotherhood is that the latter has morphed in order to engage with modernity rather than

23 M. A. S. Abdel Haleem, *The Qur'an: A new Translation* (New York: Oxford University Press, 2010), 268.
24 Mark Durie, "Salafis and the Muslim Brotherhood: What is the difference?" *Middle East Forum* (June 6, 2013); meforum.org.
25 Walter M. Weiss, *Islam: An Illustrated Historical Overview* (Hauppauge, NY: Barron's Educational Series, Inc., 2000), 162.

reject it. An Anglican vicar in Melbourne, Australia, and an associate fellow at the Middle East Forum, Mark Durie explains:

> The Brotherhood is more deceptive in language and appearance than Salafis. Salafis tend to be separatist and can give the impression of being focused upon personal religious piety, which separates them from those who do not share their beliefs. Salafis also tend to speak using pious religious jargon, making few concessions to the communicative norms of others. This is mirrored in their manner of dress, which concedes nothing to secular fashion sense. In contrast, the Brotherhood's approach is to penetrate and transform Western institutions, with the ultimate aim of bringing about the same end as the Salafis. . . .
>
> Consistent with its goal of penetration and transformation, Brotherhood ideology interacts directly with and challenges western thought. It is positive about modern science, and has developed ideological positions on challenges posed by modern economic and political realities. It has strong appeal to and actively recruits Muslim professionals and intellectuals, including doctors and scientists—many of them western-educated—who have contributed many of its leaders, and when it is powerful the Brotherhood can function as a state within a state, with its own constitution, educational system, and laws.[26]

Fundamentalism and Terrorism

Is fundamentalism unique to Islam? In her book, *Islam: A Short History*, Karen Armstrong assures us that it is not:

> The Western media often give the impression that the embattled and occasionally violent form of religiosity known as "fundamentalism" is a purely Islamic phenomenon. This is not the case. Fundamentalism is a global fact and has surfaced in every major faith in response to the problems of our modernity. There is fundamentalist Judaism, fundamentalist Christianity, fundamentalist Hinduism, fundamentalist Buddhism, fundamentalist Sikhism, and even fundamentalist Confucianism.[27]

26   Mark Durie, ibid.
27   Karen Armstrong, *Islam: A Short History* (New York, NY: Random House, 2000), 164.

Not everyone likes the term *fundamentalism* to be used for Islam. For instance, John L. Esposito, the author of *Islamic Threat: Myth or Reality?* prefers the terms *Islamic revivalism* or *Islamic activism* instead:

> First, all those who call for a return to foundational beliefs or the *fundamentals* of a religion may be called fundamentalists. . . . Second, our understanding and perceptions of fundamentalism are heavily influenced by American Protestantism. . . . For many liberal or mainline Christians, "fundamentalism" is pejorative or derogatory. . . . Third, "fundamentalism" is often equated with political activism, extremism, fanaticism, terrorism, and anti-Americanism. . . . Yet, while some engage in radical religiopolitics, most . . . work within the established order.[28]

However unfair the term may be, *fundamentalism* has become the common vernacular for many movements. Yet, though there may be minor fundamentalist movements in many religions, as Armstrong points out above, the size and strength of this worldview in Islam has positioned it as the primary religion that is resisting modernity.

One famous example of this in the last few years took place in Pakistan. The literacy rate for girls has been significantly lower than that of boys—45 percent compared to 69 percent in 2009. On October 9, 2012, a man who was part of the fundamentalist group known as the Taliban targeted and shot a fourteen-year-old girl named Malala Yousafzi in the head, because she was actively promoting education for women and publicly denouncing the Taliban's efforts to hold women back. Malala did not die, and when she recovered, she used her newfound fame to continue promoting women's education. She received the Nobel Peace Prize in 2014.[29]

In Islam, when it comes to the ideology that produces acts of terror, the morphing from fundamentalist to radical to terrorist seems to take place at an unprecedented rate around the world today. There is no other religion as likely as Islam to produce terrorists in

28 John L. Esposito, *Islamic Threat: Myth or Reality? Third Edition* (New York, NY: Oxford University Press, 1999), 5–6.
29 Sara Kettler, "Malala Yousafzai Biography," biography.com (accessed April 24, 2016).

the entire world in these modern times. Of course, there are Muslim apologists who will debate this, and there are politicians who may try to be "politically correct" by pointing to the acts of the Christians in the Crusades (which happened a thousand years ago, and which I will discuss later in this book). Or they may use the strategy of exposing some bizarre bit of modern terrorist activity conducted by a non-Muslim (yes, it happens). On the whole, however, there is simply no comparison of these bizarre freak and random incidents to the plethora of acts of brutal terror that are carried out weekly around the world by radicalized Islamic individuals or Islamic terrorist cell groups against innocent civilians and those who cannot protect themselves.

By way of illustration, BBC News tracked jihadist activities during the month of November 2014, and they concluded that 664 attacks had resulted in more than 5,000 people being killed.[30] According to the Religion of Peace, an organization which tracks incidents of deadly violence committed out of a perceived religious duty to Islam, in 2014 there were 3,001 Islamic attacks in 55 countries in which 32,863 people were killed and 27,522 were injured.[31] In February 2015, the world watched in horror as the Islamic State of Iraq and Syria (ISIS) released a video of them beheading twenty-one Coptic Christians.[32]

In January 2015, Islamic terrorists attacked the Charlie Hebdo newspaper offices in Paris, France, killing twelve, and then, in November, numerous locations in Paris, including the Bataclan Theater, were targeted by suicide bombers and terrorists with guns in what became the deadliest attack on Paris since WWII. One hundred thirty people were killed, and many more were injured.

In December 2015, in San Bernardino, California, fourteen people were killed and seventeen were injured by a Muslim man and his wife while they were attending an office Christmas party. Since

---

30 "Jihadism: Tracking a month of deadly attacks," *BBC News* (December 11, 2014); bbc.com.

31 "List of Islamic Terror: 2014"; thereligionofpeace.com (accessed April 24, 2016).

32 William M. Welch, "Christian hostages beheaded in Islamic State video," *USA Today* (February 16, 2015); usatoday.com.

1972, the Religion of Peace cites seventy-one such incidents in America in which people were killed due to Islamic fundamentalism. Most of these incidents resulted in the deaths of just one or two victims and therefore went rather unnoticed—as compared to the atrocities of 9/11, the Fort Hood massacre of 2009, the Boston Marathon bombing of 2013, or the Christmas party attack in San Bernardino.[33]

Do you know someone who has been attacked in this way? I do. It seems that the world is getting smaller, and we are all more interconnected today. So when terrorist attacks from fundamentalist groups of Islam occur, there is a growing chance that we will eventually know someone who was personally impacted. For example, in the Lahore Easter bombing in Pakistan, on March 27, 2016, a splinter group of the Taliban called the Jamaat-ul-Ahrar, identified Christians to be their main target. At least seventy-four people were killed in a park by a suicide bombing—this included Muslims, as well. I personally know and work with two of the pastors who either lost relatives or people from their congregation. In another instance, my family has been supporting a husband and wife pastoral team in Paris for years—two of my daughters have lived with them and have even served in their church at different times. One of the Paris attacks in 2015 took place right next to their church. And yet another example of my personal life being touched by terrorism was at the Boston Marathon bombing on April 15, 2013, when several bombs exploded just near the finish line. My daughter-in-law is a physical therapist, and she was actually treating runners in the medical tent only a hundred yards or so from where the bombs exploded. The medical tent in which she was serving people immediately became a triage center to save people's lives, with doctors, nurses, and even therapists doing whatever they could to help.

Why would a Muslim strap a bomb on and commit suicide in order to kill others? Traditionally, Islamic teachers claim that the Koran forbids suicide. However, the idea of being a suicide assassin in Islam is actually very old. A case in point was a group known as

---

33 "Islamic Terror on American Soil," *The Religion of Peace*; thereligionofpeace. com (accessed April 24, 2016).

the *fida'iyun*, which stands for "ready for sacrifice." In the twelfth century, in the Mediterranean area, members of this group would target certain political leaders to be assassinated. These leaders could have been Jewish, Christian, or even opposing Muslim leaders whom they did not like. After a rigorous training period in combat arms, the assassins would then get high on *hashish*, a psychoactive drug extracted from the cannabis plant, and then they would go out to carry out the assassinations with knives, swords, and spears. These assassins were assured that when they themselves were killed for their actions, they would receive great honor from Allah and the pleasure of many beautiful women fulfilling their every sexual fantasy.

Today, weapons like dynamite can do a lot more damage, and it is not just leaders who are targeted. Any group, including innocent citizens, can be killed in order to create unrest and havoc and ultimately achieve the dominance of Islam in a region.

One nation that frequently receives the brunt from fundamentalist Islamic groups is Israel. They have had many wars since 1948, and many enemies from various Islamic ranks have targeted them with terrorist attacks over the years. One of these terrorist groups is the Hezbollah (aka the Lebanese Party of God Movement). It is a Shi'a Islamist militant group and a political party based in Lebanon. Their tactics, honed in the 1990s, for training and recruitment placement reveal part of the psychology that goes into this form of warfare. Suicide bombers were trained in military ranks with mock bombs strapped to their bodies. Members regarded "self-martyrdom" as the only way to fight back against the "infidels." They practiced terrorist maneuvers that would put them within close proximity of Israeli personnel and armored vehicles before then pulling the pin on the grenades or bombs strapped to their bodies. One man defended this suicidal practice by saying, "They don't consider it suicide, because they value their lives."

The Hezbollah party exalted these individuals by hanging their pictures on city streets—with startling effect. One little boy said he wanted to be a martyr just like his father, in order to kill the "Zionist enemy" and drive them out of their land. Another man, only twenty years old, was heralded as a hero after blowing himself up along with many Israeli soldiers. In a video message to his family, he instructed them to receive congratulations rather than condolences.

The Modern Arab Crisis

Centuries before the Muslim Brotherhood was founded in Egypt; Islamic fundamentalism was flourishing in eighteenth-century Arabia, due to an alliance between Muhammad ibn Abd al-Wahhab, a fundamentalist preacher, and Muhammad ibn Saud, a militant chief of the house of Saud. From early on in Islamic history, Arabia, the place where Islam began, was not the true center seat of Islam. Ibn Wahhab desired to see Islam purified and returned to the religion of the prophet, with Mecca and Medina in Arabia restored to their rightful places in Islam. However, few converts came from his preaching, until he allied himself with a warrior who had a great ambition for power. Through military and terrorist activities, together they brought many converts to Ibn Wahhab's view of Islam. The adherents of Wahhabism today prefer to be called *Unitarians*.

Over 250 years have passed since then, and this Arabia, now called Saudi Arabia, is still ruled by the Saudi monarchy, the Koran, and puritan dogma. From Ibn Wahhab's teachings sprouted the present Wahhabism movement, which is a part of Salafism. It was fundamental to its core. The greatest differences between then and now, however, are the potency of the weapons that they use.

In his book *Crisis in Belief*, Bishop Stephen Neill points out the incredible transformation of Islamic power in the last century:

> In two generations the situation of the Islamic World has entirely changed. In 1918 it was at its lowest point of humiliation—poor, exhausted, and at almost every point subject to Christian domination. In 1978 it stood before the world, free, aggressive, and with a new sense of confidence.[34]

Since WWII, many Islamic nations have gained their independence. European colonialism ended, and the new Islamic

---

34 Stephen Neill, *Crisis in Belief* (London: Hodder and Stoughton, 1984), 61.

countries faced an identity crisis that continues to this day—often producing bloodshed, rebellion, and great social upheaval. A large portion of the continuing crisis is caused by the extremist views of the Islamic fundamentalists.

Since the time of the attack on America on September 11, 2001, there have been numerous wars fought in response to and concerning the rise of Islamic fundamentalism. America went to war in both Afghanistan (2001–2014) and Iraq (2003–2011), but there have also been various wars within Islamic countries themselves—especially between the Sunni and Shia elements. These wars, along with continual, ongoing terrorist attacks, keep many countries on edge and posed for future war. The formation of ISIS (the Islamic State of Iraq and Syria), or ISIL (the Islamic State of Iraq and the Levant), has brought a new global reality of tension between the democratic nations of the world and Islamic jihadism that has shifted the balance of power.

In his article "The Barbarians Within our Gates," Hisham Melhem, the Washington bureau chief of Al-Arabiya, wrote about the rise of the Islamic State out of the collapse of the Arab civilizations:

> Arab civilization, such as we knew it, is all but gone. The Arab world today is more violent, unstable, fragmented and driven by extremism—the extremism of the rulers and those in opposition—than at any time since the collapse of the Ottoman Empire a century ago. Every hope of modern Arab history has been betrayed. The promise of political empowerment, the return of politics, the restoration of human dignity heralded by the season of Arab uprisings in their early heydays—all have given way to civil wars, ethnic, sectarian and regional divisions and the reassertion of absolutism, both in its military and atavistic forms. With the dubious exception of the antiquated monarchies and emirates of the Gulf—which for the moment are holding out against the tide of chaos—and possibly Tunisia, there is no recognizable legitimacy left in the Arab world. . . .
>
> . . . The jihadists of the Islamic State . . . did not emerge from nowhere. They climbed out of a rotting, empty hulk—what was

left of a broken-down civilization. They are a gruesome manifestation of a deeper malady afflicting Arab political culture, which was stagnant, repressive and patriarchal after the decades of authoritarian rule that led to the disastrous defeat in the 1967 war with Israel. . . . That defeat sounded the death knell of Arab nationalism and the resurgence of political Islam, which projected itself as the alternative to the more secular ideologies that had dominated the Arab republics since the Second World War. If Arab decline was the problem, then "Islam is the solution," the Islamists said—and they believed it. . . .

. . . At their core, both political currents—Arab nationalism and Islamism—are driven by atavistic impulses and a regressive outlook on life that is grounded in a mostly mythologized past. Many Islamists, including Egypt's Muslim Brotherhood (the wellspring of such groups)—whether they say it explicitly or hint at it—are still on a ceaseless quest to resurrect the old Ottoman Caliphate. Still more radical types—the Salafists—yearn for a return to the puritanical days of Prophet Muhammad and his companions. For most Islamists, democracy means only majoritarian rule, and the rule of sharia law, which codifies gender inequality and discrimination against non-Muslims. And let's face the grim truth: There is no evidence whatever that Islam in its various political forms is compatible with modern democracy.[35]

Lessons on the Road to Damascus

The book of Acts tells the history of a Pharisee named Saul of Tarsus (later named Paul) who arrested, persecuted, and literally put Christians to death. As far as those people were concerned, he was a first-century terrorist. Yet, while he was on his way to the city of Damascus, he was confronted by the Lord. This encounter changed his perspective, his life, and his destiny. Here is part of what he experienced:

As he journeyed he came near Damascus, and suddenly a light shone around him from heaven. Then he fell to the ground, and

---

35 Hisham Melhem, "The Barbarians within our Gates," *Politico* (September 18, 2014); www.politico.com/magazine/story/2014/09/the-barbarians-within-our-gates-111116.

heard a voice saying to him, "Saul, Saul, why are you persecuting Me?" And he said, "Who are You, Lord?" Then the Lord said, "I am Jesus, whom you are persecuting. It is hard for you to kick against the goads." So he, trembling and astonished, said, "Lord, what do You want me to do?" Then the Lord said to him, "Arise and go into the city, and you will be told what you must do." —Acts 9:3–6

This same experience left Saul blind for three days, and it was not until he had gone into Damascus and had waited upon the Lord Jesus, that the Lord sent a prophet named Ananias to him. God had given Saul the vision of a man named Ananias coming to him, laying hands upon his eyes, and restoring his sight. This was a great confirmation to Saul, and through Ananias's ministry, Saul regained his sight and was baptized into the Christian faith. After a period of serving the Lord, Saul's name was changed, and he became known as the apostle Paul. He took many missionary journeys for the Lord and wrote much of the New Testament.

In Acts 26, this same Damascus-road experience was described by Paul many years later, as he testified before King Agrippa. Paul recognized the event as the single-most-impactful turning point in his life. Many of us who come to Christ later in our lives have such a turning point, a moment in time when we recognize that Jesus is trying to get our attention and we are overwhelmed by His presence.

The reference in the passage above to "*kick against the goads*" has to do with ox prods. An ox prod was a stick with a sharp, pointed piece of iron on the end of it. When an unruly, rebellious ox kicked out, it would hurt the beast and hopefully bring it into submission to its master. In this case, Jesus was the Master speaking to Paul. In truth, Jesus is the Master of the entire universe. He is the King of heaven! He is the King of the entire earth!

A king must have a kingdom. The New Testament says much about the Kingdom of God. Jesus is the King of the Kingdom of God. Paul learned to stop kicking against the goads and to serve his Master as he was instructed to do. Indeed, kingdoms have ambassadors, who have the authority of the king to make decisions in foreign lands. Paul was made an ambassador of Jesus (see Ephesians 6:20; 2 Corinthians 5:20).

We learn from Paul's road-to-Damascus experience that Jesus will sometimes confront terrorists with His presence. And if they turn to Him, Jesus can use them to share the Gospel message of the Kingdom of God with other people. There are modern-day terrorists who have encountered the Lord Jesus Christ and have had their perspectives, their lives, and their eternal destinies changed.

One such modern-day example is a man named Al-Rashid, who was the leader of a fundamentalist Islamic group that aimed to terrorize Christians. Much like Saul, he was angry at any Muslims who converted to Christ, so he decided to target a pastor who had been a former Muslim. Al-Rashid had a twisted plan to kill the pastor's family and thus force the pastor to renounce Christ and turn back to Islam. However, his attempts to assassinate the pastor's family members kept failing, because of what appeared to be divine intervention. Eventually he was successful in poisoning one of the children, the pastor's daughter, and she became very sick. A reporter who later interviewed Rashid asked him to explain what happened next:

> "I was watching with two others from an ambulance near the hospital to see his daughter's death. Our plan was to kidnap her dead body along with his family in our ambulance," Rashid recounts. Then something happened that amazed Rashid. "I saw a ball of light come down from the sky and stand over the room where his daughter was lying unconscious," he says. To his utter disbelief, he watched a hand come from the ball of light, touch the pastor's daughter, and she immediately regained consciousness and stood up. He was astonished to see a hole in the middle of the hand and that blood was flowing down. "I trembled with fear," Rashid says. "I felt giddy and fell down. My friends moved me from there at once."[36]

After the pastor's daughter was miraculously healed, Rashid had a troubling vision of Jesus and His nailed hand. Shortly thereafter, he got ahold of a Bible, and as he opened it, his eyes saw the passage in John 1:9–10, which says: "That was the true Light which gives

---

36 Mark Ellis, "Islamic Terrorist Hunted a Pastor Until Jesus Gave Him an Unusual Vision," *Charisma News* (April 21, 2016); charismanews.com.

light to every man coming into the world. He was in the world, and the world was made through Him, and the world did not know Him." Rashid's heart of understanding was opened at that moment, to recognize that the Light he had seen was Jesus.

Eventually, he sought out the very pastor whose family he had tried to kill, and that pastor led him in a salvation prayer. Rashid was baptized and received the gift of the Holy Spirit.

Today, he is one of the key leaders in a ministry that makes the Bible available to Muslims in the Middle East. Rashid, like the apostle Paul, submitted to the true Master, who was then able to use him to build people up rather than destroy them.

PART TWO

THE HISTORICAL ROOTS OF

ISLAM

————— ✡ ✝ ☪ —————

Chapter 3

It All Started with Abraham

Had Abraham not had faith, then Sarah would surely have died of sorrow, and Abraham, dull with grief, instead of understanding the fulfilment, would have smiled at it as at a youthful dream. But Abraham believed, and therefore he was young; for he who always hopes for the best becomes old, deceived by life, and he who is always prepared for the worst becomes old prematurely; but he who has faith, retains eternal youth.[37]

—Søren Kierkegaard

Abraham

Abraham, the patriarch of our faith, is an important figure in the religious history of Christians, Jews, and Muslims. Interestingly, at least one translation of the Koran states that Abraham was a Muslim, even though Islam would not even arise for at least 2,500 years after Abraham's life. "Abraham was neither Jew nor Christian; but he was sound in faith, a Muslim; and not of those who add gods to God" (Sura 3:60).[38] Another translation of this sura puts it this way: "Abraham was neither Jew nor Christian. He was upright and devoted to God, never an idolater."[39] A better understanding of why Abraham's

---

37 Søren Kierkegaard, *Fear and Trembling* (London, England: Penguin Books, 2006), 18.
38 *The Koran*, J. M. Rodwell, trans. (Rutland, VT: Charles E. Tuttle Co., Inc., 1994), 37.
39 *The Qur'an*, 39.

ancestral connection is so important to Islam can be gained from a review of his life as recorded in the Bible.

We first read about Abram (later to be called Abraham) in the biblical book of *Genesis*. God called him to leave his country and family and move to a new land. There, God would bless him, make him into a great nation, bless those who blessed him, and curse those who cursed him—and in Abram, "all the families of the earth shall be blessed" (Genesis 12:3 NKJV).

When he arrived in Canaan, God promised him, "To your descendants I will give this land" (Genesis 12:7 NKJV). However, Abram confessed his fears to the Lord, telling Him that one of his servants would have to be the heir, because he had no son of his own. Yet the Lord told him that the servant's son would not be his heir, but rather, one who would come from his own body (see Genesis 15:4). Abram was seventy-five years old, but he was learning that God's plans are not fulfilled through man's efforts. They are fulfilled through His grace and in His time.

> Then He brought him outside and said, "Look now toward heaven, and count the stars if you are able to number them." And He said to him, "So shall your descendants be." And he believed in the LORD, and He accounted it to him for righteousness. —Genesis 15:5–6 NKJV

Time passed, and there was still no son for Abram. His wife, Sarai, was barren. So, out of desperation, she told Abram to take her servant, Hagar, and conceive a son through her. Abram did so, and Hagar conceived a son when Abram was eighty-six.

The pregnancy caused great difficulties between the two women, Sarai and Hagar, her maidservant. Finally, Hagar fled from Sarai's jealousy and anger, escaping to the wilderness. God heard her cries and appeared to her. He told her to return to Sarai and submit to her authority. He also said that the name of Hagar's son would be *Ishmael,* meaning "God will hear." God assured Hagar that Ishmael's descendants would be tremendous—too many to count, in fact. In addition, He proclaimed a prophecy regarding Ishmael's character:

"Behold, you are with child,
And you shall bear a son.
You shall call his name Ishmael,
Because the LORD has heard your affliction.
He shall be a wild man;His hand shall be against every man,
And every man's hand against him.
And he shall dwell in the presence of
all his brethren." —Genesis 16:11–12 NKJV

Hagar returned to Abram's household and submitted to Sarai and her husband. God still had His plan. In order to prepare Abram and Sarai's hearts for the coming of their own son, as He had promised, God spoke to them and changed their names:

> Then God said to Abraham, "As for Sarai your wife, you shall not call her name Sarai, but Sarah shall be her name. And I will bless her and also give you a son by her; then I will bless her, and she shall be a mother of nations; kings of peoples shall be from her."
> Then Abraham fell on his face and laughed, and said in his heart, "Shall a child be born to a man who is one hundred years old? And shall Sarah, who is ninety years old, bear a child? And Abraham said to God, "Oh, that Ishmael might live before You!"
> Then God said: "No, Sarah your wife shall bear you a son, and you shall call his name Isaac; I will establish My covenant with him for an everlasting covenant and with his descendants after him.
> "And as for Ishmael, I have heard you. Behold, I have blessed him, and will make him fruitful, and will multiply him exceedingly. He shall beget twelve princes, and I will make him a great nation.
> "But My covenant I will establish with Isaac, whom Sarah shall bear to you at this set time next year." —Genesis 17:15–21 NKJV

Just as the Lord promised, the next year Isaac was born to Abraham and to Sarah in their old age, and history favored Abraham as the "father of faith." The name *Isaac* actually means "laughter," and it appears that the Lord chose that name in response to Abraham's laughter when he heard the Lord was going to give him and Sarah a son in their old age. When Sarah first heard the plan, she laughed, as well. Yet, soon their laughter turned into cries of joy, when the son they had been promised was born (see Genesis 18:12–15; 21:6).

Ishmael

> "He shall be a wild man;
> His hand shall be against every man,
> And every man's hand against him.
> And he shall dwell in the presence of all his brethren." —Genesis 16:12 NKJV

The Hebrew words used in this passage for "wild man" are *pere' adam. Adam,* in Hebrew, is obviously translated as "man"; and *pere'* gives the sense of "running wild." Out of the ten times this term is used in the Old Testament, nine times it refers specifically to the trait of a stubborn, independent, or untamed ass.[40] The tenth, and only other reference, is used in this description of Ishmael. This prophecy refers not only to Ishmael himself, but also to all of his sons and to all of their descendants, namely the Ishmaelites, who became nomadic Bedouins and wandering Arabs.[41]

It is interesting that the word *Adam* in Hebrew means "man," and that God called Ishmael a "wild man." Let's consider this in light of the first man, who was named Adam. In Genesis 2, God created Adam. He was given the job of caring for the Garden of Eden. He named the animals. Eventually, God saw that Adam was lonely, so He created Eve to be Adam's wife. They had access to all of the Garden, and they were given the freedom to eat from the fruit of any tree (Genesis 2:16–17)—except the tree of the knowledge of good and evil. This tree represented not only a test of their obedience and faithfulness to God, but also, their choice to eat from it represented the abandonment of the close relational position that they held with God in the Garden. The immediate love and goodness that flowed from Him, including His influence on their innocent purity and wisdom, would immediately be halted.

---

40 James Strong, *The New Strong's Exhaustive Concordance of the Bible* (Nashville, TN: Thomas Nelson Publishers, 1995), 1523–1524.

41 Adam Clarke, *Adam Clarke's Commentary on the Holy Bible* (Grand Rapids, MI: Baker Book House, 1987), 39.'s

Genesis 3 contains the sad story of when Adam and Eve ate of the Tree of the Knowledge of Good and Evil, after Eve was deceived by the serpent. What was the result? First, Adam and Eve suddenly recognized their own nakedness, and they saw that their relationship with each other had been irrevocably altered. So, they attempted to cover themselves with leaves from the plants in the Garden. Second, the very first emotions of guilt and shame were experienced as they hid from God, knowing that their relationship with Him had also been altered forever. Third, blame shifting occurred, as the man blamed the woman and the woman blamed the serpent. The bliss of Paradise was thrown into pandemonium, and a judgment filled with curses was the result. Adam and Eve could not remain in the Garden of Eden, lest they eat of the Tree of Life and remain forever in their sins, but before they were driven out, God graciously clothed them in tunics of skin—made from the bodies of innocent animals. This represented the first sacrifice in the Bible, and it was symbolic of the future coming of the Lamb of God, Jesus, who would one day be sacrificed for the sins of the whole world (see John 1:29).

After Adam and Eve were driven from the Garden of Eden, they conceived and bore two sons, Cain and Abel. Genesis 4 reveals the tragedy of the first murder on earth, when Cain chose to kill his brother, Abel, because of his impulsive nature and his jealousy. This undoubtedly represents the evil part of the character that came from eating the fruit of the Tree of the Knowledge of Good and Evil.

With regard to Ishmael, then, what can be derived from the prophecy that refers to him as a *"wild man,"* or, to be more in line with this context, a *"wild Adam"*? Since the word *wild* has the idea of a baser animal nature behind it, the idea of savage animal that kills out of impulse or even jealousy, striving with the other animals for position or benefit, comes to mind. Let us compare Ishmael's character to that of Cain's. Just as Cain killed Abel because his offering of fruit was not valued by the Lord as was Abel's sacrifice of the firstborn of his flock (see Genesis 4:1–12), it would appear that Ishmael's relationship with Isaac, who was the chosen one of God, was not the best of sibling relationships. If Ishmael's hand was truly against every man, starting with his own brother, Isaac, then murder was in his heart, just as it was in Cain's.

As Isaac and Ishmael grew up together, contention broke out between them. Ishmael was seen "scoffing" at Isaac (see Genesis 21:9). This demonstrates his jealousy. And so Sarah asked Abraham to send Hagar and Ishmael away—and Abraham did so. Because Ishmael was also a son of Abraham, the Lord assured Abraham that the boy would someday become a great nation in and of himself (see Genesis 21:8–21).

In Genesis 25:13–15, we are told that Ishmael's twelve sons lived to the east of the Hebrews. The Ishmaelites became nomadic tribes that wandered throughout the region of northern Arabia. The Jewish historian Josephus described them as an "Arabian nation."[42] Today, many Muslims claim Ishmael as their direct ancestor, and they believe that all of Arabia descended from him. Others, more accurately, claim that many people groups came together to comprise the peoples of Arabia. Biblical evidence reveals that Abraham had other offspring after Sarah's death. His second wife, Keturah, gave him many other children. And before his death, Abraham gave gifts to each of his heirs and sent them eastward, away from his son Isaac (see Genesis 25:6).

One local legend tells us that Hagar and Ishmael originally settled in the city of Mecca. Abraham once visited them there and helped Ishmael to rebuild the Kabah, a cube-style building that, according to Islamic teaching, had originally been erected by Adam himself, but had fallen into disrepair.[43] The Kabah was the local temple of Mecca, a very important site of worship for the community and for pilgrims who journeyed there.

The World and the Early Life of Muhammad

Almost 2,600 years after the lifetimes of Abraham and Ishmael, Muhammad, the founder of Islam, was born in Mecca on the Arabi-

---

42 *Josephus: Complete Works*, W. Whiston trans. (Grand Rapids, MI: Kregel Publications, 1980), 36.
43 Armstrong, 17.

an Peninsula. He was supposedly a direct descendant from Ishmael. And throughout his life, he exhibited similar characteristics to those that Ishmael possessed.

Muhammad was born in CE 570 to Abdullah (Abd-Allah) and his mother, Aminah. Legend says that on the night of his birth, a star illuminated the heavens and that his umbilical cord was severed by Providence—without human aid.[44] As a child, two angels supposedly visited him. They opened his breast with their bare hands and literally washed his heart with snow until it was as pure as a crystal.[45]

At that time, the vast Arabian Peninsula was in a lull following warfare that had raged for decades between two great empires to the north. The Zoroastrian/Persian Empire stretched from Iraq to Afghanistan, and the Christian/Byzantine Empire was comprised of Asia Minor, Syria, Egypt, Abyssinia, and southeast Europe.[46] The religious and political struggles over the Arabian Peninsula had exhausted the people and drained the resources of each of these empires. For the time being, while Muhammad grew into adulthood, peace reigned. In his thought-provoking book *In the Shadow of the Prophet: The Struggle for the Soul of Islam*, author Milton Viorst states: "In time the wars in Arabia would resume, but the attackers would be Muhammad's followers, seeking to establish their new faith, before turning their attention to Byzantine and Persian conquerors."[47]

In the time of Muhammad's childhood, while the two empires were not fighting over the peninsula, there were many other different skirmishes among the tribes of Arabia itself. Survival demanded loyalty, discipline, and vigilance to one's own tribe.[48] Some historians believe there was a great population explosion in the Bedouin

44 Carson Herrington, *Arts of the Islamic World: A Teacher's Guide* (Washington, D.C.: Smithsonian Institute, 2002), 6.
45 Weiss, 12.
46 Anne Cooper, *Ishmael, My Brother: A Christian Introduction to Islam* (Crowborough, England: Monarch Publications, 1997), 102.
47 Milton Viorst, *In the Shadow of the Prophet: The Struggle for the Soul of Islam* (Cambridge, MA: Westview Press, 2001), 79.
48 Viorst, 78.

communities at that time that ultimately stressed the limited water and food resources that existed there. So, this group of wanderers were forced to become more urbanized.

Muhammad was born into the Quraysh tribe, the preeminent line of traders in Mecca. His father was part of the Hashim clan of the Quraysh tribe. However, before Muhammad was born, his father died, and his mother passed away when he was only six.[49] Historical accounts claim that Muhammad's mother practiced occultism, had spiritualistic visions, and claimed that spirits, or jinn, visited her throughout her lifetime.[50]

After her death, the boy Muhammad lived with his grandfather, who was the guardian of the Kabah temple.[51] A strong bond of love formed between them. Unfortunately, after only two years, when Muhammad was eight years old, his grandfather died. The boy was subsequently passed around to relatives and eventually landed in the custody of his poor uncle, Abu Talib. Muhammad became accustomed to living simply throughout these meager years, and he went to work at an early age. There is some disagreement over whether Muhammad received any education as a child. He did, however, receive training in the weapons of war.[52]

At this time, Mecca was an important and thriving center of trade, and caravans constantly passed through the city. It was described as a place where "no waters flow . . . not a blade of grass on which to rest the eye . . . only merchants there."[53]

The Religious Culture

At the time of Muhammad's life, the religious system was varied. Several monotheistic cults had been established in southern Arabia, including one devoted to al-Rahman, "the merciful." Later, that

49 Ibid.

50 Robert Morey, *The Islamic Invasion: Confronting the World's Fastest Growing Religion* (Eugene, OR: Harvest House, 1992), 50. The author refers to Alfred Guillaume, *Islam* (London: Penguin Books, 1954), 71.

51 Cooper, 104.

52 Ibid., 105.

53 Virost, 78, quoting Peters, *Muhammad*, 23.

name was to gain prominence in the Koran as a favorite description of Allah.[54] There was also a group known as the *Hanifs* (Arabic for "the upright"), who claimed they were the spiritual descendants of Abraham and who ascribed to the worship of a single, highly personal deity. And the Bedouins essentially believed that fate ruled their destiny.

Throughout the Arabian Peninsula, there was a vast amount of idolatry taking place at that time. Many gods and idols were worshiped, and there was a great sense of restlessness in Mecca as a result. The Arabs knew that the religions of Judaism and Christianity had a longer history than Islam, and thus they were more sophisticated than their own beliefs and rituals. As a result, some of the Quraysh tribe had come to believe that the "high god" of their pantheon, *al-Lah*, was essentially the same deity who was worshiped by the Jews and the Christians.[55]

The origin of the name *Allah* and when worship to him began is hotly debated today, even among Christians. There are many theories but two stand out. First, there are a group of scholars who contend that the name *Allah* is how both Jewish and Christian Aramaic speakers referred to God prior to the time of Muhammad. It is also the name used by modern Jewish and Christian Arabic speakers because that is the only word that there is in their language for God. Some etymologists think the word *Allah*, which means "the god," was borrowed from the ancient Aramaic word *elahh*. The term *elahh* can be found in the Bible—in Ezra 4:24 and Daniel 6:23 and elsewhere. Second, other scholars oppose the Aramaic connection claiming that the name was derived from the term *al-ilah*. This term was used by the Sabaeans, a people in South Arabia, as a title of respect for their moon god named *Sin*. The term *al-ilah* also means "the god."

When weighing which of these origin theories is most likely the correct one, it should be noted that the ninth century Christian scholar and apologist, Abd al-Masih al-Kindy, in his defense of

---

54 Alan Jones, *Introduction to the Koran* (Rutland, VT: Charles E. Tuttle Co., Inc., 1994), xi–xii.
55 Armstrong, 3.

Christianity against Islam, asserted that the Muslims borrowed the name of Allah from the Sabaean moon god Sin. He was very knowledgeable of Arab customs. Abd al-Masih al-Kindy, who lived in that region of the world close to the time that Islam began, probably had a clearer understanding of the pre-Islamic origin of the name *Allah*. Since there is evidence that the Sabaeans did worship a moon god and they did live in South Arabia, there is a strong connection for the theory that the name *Allah* came from the term *al-ilah*.

As was the case in many ancient cultures, a pantheon of deities was usually headed up by one primary god. Leading pantheons from other cultures included:

- Egyptians: Atum
- Ugarit: El
- Greeks: Zeus
- Assyrian: Assur
- Romans: Jupiter
- Babylonian: Ea
- Phoenicians: Baal
- Sumer: Enlil

There were also numerous other deities that were male and female couples, such as Baal and Astarte; El and Athirat; and Zeus and Hera. Most ancient regions, cities, and tribes served their own patron deity, which, to them, presided over the others. This system of idol worship had been around for eons.[56]

Most early cultures, including much of the Ancient Near East, worshiped the moon as a female deity and the sun as a male deity. However, it was the reverse among the Arabs. Muhammad's tribe, the Quraysh, was particularly devoted to Allah, the moon deity, and

---

56 Marc van de Mieroop explains that in ancient cultures, this was popular. For instance, each city in Sumer had a primary deity associated with it. Nippur was associated with the deity Enlil; Ur with Nanna; and Girsu with Ningirsu. The same phenomena took place all over the ancient world—except among the Jews and Christians, who served only one God. *The Ancient Mesopotamian City* (Oxford, England: Oxford University Press, 1999), 46.

his daughters. Author Robert Morey, in his book *The Islamic Invasion*, makes an interesting observation:

> In Arabia, the sun god was viewed as a female goddess and the moon as the male god. As has been pointed out by many scholars, such as Alfred Guilluame, the moon god was called by various names, one of which was Allah! The name of Allah was used as a personal name of the moon god, in addition to other titles that could be given to him.
>
> Allah, the moon god, was married to the sun goddess. Together they produced three goddesses, who were called the "daughters of Allah." These three goddesses were called Al-Lat, Al-Uzza, and Manat.[57]

However, it would appear that Muhammad came to the belief that Allah, the high-god of the Quraysh tribe, was the Creator of all. In Sura 41:37 of the Koran, Muhammad told his followers not to worship the sun or the moon but God only.

It is of note that our own English word *God* possibly had pagan origins. However, when people use it, they don't think about its origins but only that it refers to God Almighty. It is the same with those today who use the term *Allah*.

Muhammad and the Koran

Muhammad grew up and worked as a camel driver until the age of twenty-five. At this time, he married Khadijah, a rich, older widow. Some historians say that she was fifteen years older than Muhammad. Others dispute this, because she was able to bear him seven children, which would be unlikely for a woman who was already forty at the time of her marriage. Khadijah owned a fruit business in Mecca. Muhammad assumed the responsibilities for it and ran the business for fifteen years. Marriage brought to Muhammad great wealth and social position. Of the six or seven children the couple had, each of the boys died in infancy, but four daughters survived to live into adulthood. From what we know of their marriage,

---

57 Morey, 6.

Muhammad and Khadijah had a happy, monogamous relationship for two decades, until her death.[58]

Tradition holds that in CE 610, on the seventeenth day of Ramadan, Muhammad went out to pray in a cave on Mount Hira. It was here that Gabriel, the angel of God, first acted as an intermediary, speaking the word of God to Muhammad (see sura 96). Muhammad told the people that he had been given these direct words from Allah, the one supreme god whom they should all worship.

The culture of that day was one of oral tradition, and so Muhammad's revelations were not immediately written down. Muhammad eventually had scribes write down the words, but the entire collection of his visions was not completely assembled until after his death. This collection of revelations eventually became known as the *Koran*.

Islam holds that the Koran is a *verbatim record* of God's speech. In Arabic, the word *Koran* means "recitation," implying that the text is an *exact* recitation of Allah's words to Muhammad. In order to be a Muslim, a person must believe in God's absolute authorship of the Koran as His exact words. Thus, believers in Islam must maintain that the Koran is a perfect book.

When Muhammad started his time of preaching, his probable initial intention was to simply rid his tribe of idolatry. Only later did he expand his "vision" and purposely embark on the creation of an entirely new religion. A convert to Muhammad's religion would eventually be called a *Muslim*, meaning "one who is submitted to God."

---

58 Viorst, 80.

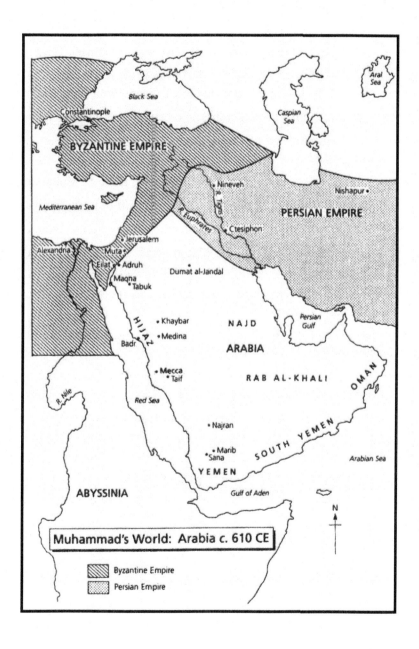

Mumammad's World: Arabia c. 610 CE

- Byzantine Empire
- Persian Empire

Timeline 1: The Rise of Islam

2000 BCE: Abraham and Hagar have a son, Ishmael. Hagar and Ishmael move east to modern Arabia.

CE 570: Muhammad is born in Mecca, on the Arabian Peninsula.

576: Muhammad's mother dies, and he moves to live with relatives.

595: Muhammad marries Khadijah and takes over her trading business.

610: The first revelations of the Koran are given to Muhammad.

612: Muhammad begins to preach. Quraysh opposition arises.

620: The Arabs secretly invite Muhammad to lead their community.

622: Muhammad moves to Medina with seventy other families, fleeing the opposition they were facing in Mecca.

624: The Battle of Badr takes place, and the Muslims defeat a Meccan caravan.

625: The Battle of Uhud takes place, and the Meccans defeat the Muslims.

627: The Battle of Ahzab takes place, and the Muslims soundly defeat the Meccans again.

628: The Treaty of Hudaybiyyah is signed between Mecca and Medina.

630: Muhammad marches on Mecca with ten thousand men and is able to conquer the city without a fight.

632: Muhammad, the Prophet of Islam dies. Abu Bakr is elected as the first caliph of the new religion of Islam.

CHAPTER *4*

Muhammad: The Prophet-Warrior

*The sword of Mahomet and the Koran are the most fatal enemies of
Civilization, Liberty, and Truth, which the world has yet known.*[59]
—William Muir

The Early Controversies

Originally, Muhammad's friends and his tribe members did not accept his revelations or his claim to be an apostle of Allah. About two years after he received his first "revelation," he started to preach his message. Yet his actions were strange for someone who was calling himself a "prophet."

When Muhammad received a "revelation," it was often accompanied by a seizure—in modern terms, the prophet was likely an epileptic. At first, due to the limited medical knowledge of that day and age, he feared that he might be possessed by a demon, and he even thought of taking his own life. However, not too long after that consideration, he had another "prophetic seizure" that instructed him *not* to commit suicide.

In his book, *Life Alert: The Medical Case of Muhammad*, Dede Korkut, MD, provides interesting evidence that Muhammad likely suffered from complex partial seizures (CPS). He states:

---

59 William Muir, *The Life of Mahomet, Volume 4* (1861), p. 322.

It has long been known and acknowledged by Muslims and non-Muslims alike that Muhammad suffered from frequent epileptic seizures. Only in comparatively recent times, however, have medical doctors gathered enough clinical evidence about the various forms of epilepsy to categorically identify the type with which Muhammad was afflicted. Modern medical knowledge is able to throw much light on the details of Muhammad's life, experiences, and compulsions, which we learn of in the Qur'an and the Hadith. This knowledge is of vital importance to anyone who desires to rightly judge Muhammad's visions, teachings, and behavior.[60]

These epileptic seizures not only caused confusion among his witnesses as to the source of Muhammad's revelations, but it has made many modern historical scholars wonder about his visions, as well. Of course, Muslims embrace Muhammad and his message in faith, but they must allow others to interpret Muhammad's revelations for themselves. Just as Muslims are free to interpret these seizures as "divine visitations," non-Muslims are free to interpret them as caused by the medical phenomena of epileptic seizures, by spiritual demonic possession, by an overactive imagination, by an elaborate con or fraud perpetrated against his fellow citizens, or by religious hysteria on the part of his followers.[61]

Muhammad's wife, Khadijah, was the first to believe in his visions and revelations. She encouraged him with regard to the visions, consistently reminding him that he was a good man, and that, therefore, the visitations must be from God and not from any demonic source. Next, his cousins Ali and Zaid and a friend named Abu Bakr joined his new religious group. His following slowly grew, but there was continuous opposition from members of the Quraysh.[62]

In order to appease the idolatrous factions in the tribe, Muhammad claimed to have had a revelation that it was acceptable to worship the three "idol daughters" of Allah: Al-Lat, Al-Uzza, and Manat. These daughters of Allah were to be exalted, and they, in turn, would

---

60 Dede Korkut, MD, *Life Alert: The Medical Case of Muhammad* (Enumclaw, WA: Winepress Publishing, 2001), ix.
61 Hurgronji, *Mohammedanism* (Westport, CT: Hyperion Press, 1981), 46.
62 Cooper, 106.

intercede to Allah on behalf of the people. This allowed the idolaters to be more open to Muhammad's apostleship. Consider this part of Sura 53, the "Sura of the star":

> Did you consider al-Lat and al-Uzza
> And al-Manat, the third, the other?
> Those are the swans exalted:
> Their intercession is expected:
> Their likes are not neglected.[63]

This particular revelation got Muhammad into a lot of trouble. This text eventually came to be known as the "satanic verses" of the Koran, because either Muhammad gave in to the temptation of Satan (*Shaitan*) to compromise his faith in the worship of one God—Allah—or Satan's influence caused Muhammad to recite something that was not from God. Could Satan be able to slip in false verses without the prophet noticing it? The implications of this would be devastating for this new monotheistic religion.

Soon, however, some of Muhammad's more faithful followers convinced the prophet to reverse this view. He did so, and the verses were altered, although they have been a point of contention and debate ever since. When Muhammad recanted this sura, tensions grew even greater between the chafed factions, because now he seemed to be proclaiming that one's absolute obedience should be given to Allah alone.

In CE 620, the prophet was secretly approached by Arabs from the settlement of Yathrib (later called Medina) and asked to lead their community. At first, Muhammad did not move to Medina immediately. He continued his work in Mecca, despite the opposition from the Quraysh.

But by CE 622, three years after both his wife and his uncle had died, the opposition to Muhammad had become so great in Mecca, that he finally decided to move. First, he went to Taif, but he found no converts there. Suras 46:29–35 and 72:1–28 tell us that, on his way back to Mecca, Muhammad preached to the jinn (genies) and

---

63 Cooper, 268.

was able to convert them to Islam. These spirits, in turn, preached the message of Islam to the people. This is likely a fictitious story, but it does reveal the prophet's shamanistic tendencies.[64]

Greatly unprepared for further contention in Mecca, Muhammad soon decided to move his religious operations to Yathrib (Medina) to avoid the continuing confrontations. His group included a community of about seventy families. Author Robert Morey estimates the significance of this move of Muhammad's with this insight: "This move was of great significance in the development of Islam. Muslims use the date of the migration, the Hijra, as the start of the Muslim era [calendar]. . . . The people were united into one single community, a brotherhood, called the *Umma* [same as *Ummah*]. The unity was no longer based on tribe, clan, or blood relationships, but on their status as believers, united by faith in the one God and Muhammad his apostle."[65]

Whereas one tribe dominated Mecca, the Quraysh, Medina was divided between two different Arab tribes: the Aus and the Kainuka. Until Muhammad's move to Medina, a longstanding feud had existed between these Arab groups. Muhammad was able to unite the city under his leadership.

Medina also was home to three Jewish tribes, as well as a Christian community. Obviously, the teachings of the Jews and Christians in Medina helped to prepare the people for Muhammad's monotheistic message. At the same time, the Jews and Christians probably supplied Muhammad with new information that he incorporated into his revelations, including such concepts as monotheism, the resurrection, and the importance of developing one authoritative document to unite the people. Also during this time in Medina, Muhammad tried to interest the Jews and Christians in his new religion. Muhammad even used the term *prophet* to describe himself to the Jews, and the word *apostle* with the Christians. However, as soon as these two groups rejected his teachings and his claims to be a "prophet" or an "apostle," enmity emerged in their relationships.

---

64 Morey, 80.
65 Ibid., 106–107.

Until this time, Muhammad's proselytizing methods had been a bit strange, but not violent. However, now his methods changed. Obtaining his visionary goal now seemed to require more than simply a spirit of prophecy; it seemed to necessitate a warrior spirit—in other words, intolerance for other religious beliefs, mixed together with a wild, barbaric spirit.

The Rise of Muhammad

During the years when Muhammad lived in Medina, several battles with the Meccans helped establish the new religion of Islam in Arabia. Muhammad first demonstrated his militant power in the Nakha raid, in which he sent men out to attack a caravan. One man from the caravan was killed, others were captured for ransom, and the caravan was looted.

In CE 624, Muhammad defeated another large caravan of Meccans who had been threatening Medina. This became known as the Battle of Badr. One year later, in the Battle of Uhud, the Meccans turned around and attacked the Muslims. At first, it appeared that the Muslims would win, but the Meccans counterattacked. The Muslims fell apart, and Muhammad was almost killed, suffering a stab wound through the mouth by a sword.

By CE 627, the Meccans had joined forces with stronger Jewish tribes in the area, and together they marched to attack Medina in what would become known as the Battle of Ahzab. However, the city had dug a large trench to protect itself.[66] The Muslims attacked their attackers and ultimately put them on the run. For this attempt to take out the Muslims, Muhammad repaid the Jewish settlements by looting and killing in their territory: "After one Jewish town had surrendered, seven hundred to one thousand men were beheaded in one day, while all the women and children were sold into slavery."[67]

After these difficult battles, a treaty was finally drawn up between Mecca and Muhammad, supposedly to protect the interests and religious beliefs of both groups for the next ten years. However, within just a few short years, Muhammad broke the treaty and marched on Mecca.

66 Cooper, 108.
67 Morey, 83.

In CE 630—and during the holy month of Ramadan—Muhammad led a great army of ten thousand men to Mecca. When the residents submitted to his invasion, he entered the city peacefully, and most of the civilians converted to Islam. The 360 idols that were positioned within the Kabah were destroyed, with the exception of the black stone, which, to Muhammad, represented Allah himself. Muhammad was now the undisputed leader of the area. Arab tribesmen flocked to him, and Islam began to spread rapidly throughout Arabia. Muhammad returned to Medina and lived there relatively peaceably, until his sudden death in CE 632 at the age of sixty-two.

Muhammad's Social Accomplishments

Muhammad brought to the Arabs a whole new religion and way of life, by providing them with the material and teachings for the Koran—a soon-to-be written, lasting testimony of Muhammad's beliefs and sayings. He was ultimately successful in uniting the Arabs behind his cause. And, as is the case with other great political and religious leaders, Muhammad was able to identify a need in the population and then sell them a vision that would give them a more systematic approach to life. This new "religious cult" flourished in the spiritual vacuum that had once existed in Arabia. And, eventually, it grew to become a major world religion.

Cults provide answers for and meet the needs of many people who are drifting through their lives and feeling lost. Cults can provide a sense of purpose, family, community, ownership, and direction toward an ultimate destiny. Of course, the problem with cults, in general, is that they actually tell people how to think—and there are serious and harsh penalties for bucking the system. All of these concepts are true within the religious cult of Islam. Muhammad established a way of life that fills virtually every waking hour of every follower's day with spiritual rituals.

The prophet's message was able to curb the archaic blood feuds that had existed between the nomadic Arabian tribes, it established a sense of spiritual equality among Muslims, it increased moral behavior due to its strict sense of law and order, and it outlined instructions for charity and helping the poor. His message encouraged monotheism by promoting the worship of only one God, the God of Abraham—who should have been named *Allah*—the supreme god of their already-existing pantheon of idolatry.

Although Muhammad did not provide for social equality among women and men, some believe that Muhammad did try to advance the poor conditions of women by improving the fairness of the marriage and divorce laws in his system of government. He also allowed women the right to receive an inheritance and the right to own property—unusual in that day and age. However, under Sharia law to this day, a daughter's inheritance is still only half that of her brother's, and in court cases, a woman's testimony is only "worth" half that of a man's. So, so much for Muhammad's supposed "advancement" of women! A wife cannot leave the house or the country without her husband's permission, and if a woman is raped, there must be four witnesses in order to convict a supposedly guilty ma; otherwise, the man usually will be set free.[68]

William Muir, a Scottish historian who specialized in studying the life and teachings of Muhammad, wrote a poignant analysis of the social accomplishments of the man:

> Some, indeed, dream of an Islam in the future, rationalized and regenerate. All this has been tried already, and has miserably failed. The Koran has so encrusted the religion in a hard, unyielding casement of ordinances and social laws, that if the shell be broken the life is gone. A rationalistic Islam would be Islam no longer. The contrast between our own faith and Islam is most remarkable. There are in our Scriptures living germs of truth, which accord with civil and religious liberty, and will expand with advancing civilization. In Islam it is just the reverse. The Koran has no such teaching as with us has abolished polygamy, slavery, and arbitrary divorce, and has elevated woman to her proper place. As a Reformer, Mahomet did advance his people to a certain point, but as a Prophet he left them fixed immovably at that

68 Michelle A. Vu, "Interview: Ex–Muslim Women on Life under Sharia Law," *Christian Post* (April 9, 2009); christianpost.com.

point for all time to come. The tree is of artificial planting. Instead of containing within itself the germ of growth and adaptation to the various requirements of time and clime and circumstance, expanding with the genial sunshine and rain from heaven, it remains the same forced and stunted thing as when first planted some twelve centuries ago.[69]

The Spiritual Problems of Muhammad's Character

Muhammad brought spiritual and social transformation to the Arabs; however, it cannot be denied that his methods and character reveal serious problems with the reliability of his teachings. After moving to Medina, the "warring" side of Muhammad's personality emerged, and he sent out Abdallah Ibn Jahsh with eight other men in order to raid a caravan. This became known as the Nakha raid, and it took place on the last day of the month of Rajab, a month considered to be extremely holy to the Arabs. It was meant to be a time of truce. Yet, Muhammad ordered it, and the raid was conducted. In it, one innocent victim was killed, and the caravan was captured.

When word got out about what he had ordered, Muhammad was accused of breaking the truce. He denied that he had given the orders for the attack during the sacred month, and he repudiated the actions of his men. He also refused to take any of the booty—at first. But later he received the revelation, later written out in Sura 2:214, that denounced the attack but justified Muhammad's taking of the loot for the "cause of Allah." In the insightful book *Mohammad: The Man and His Faith*, author Tor Andrae explains this character flaw of Muhammad: "What offends us is the calculating slyness with which he cleverly provokes Abdallah's action without assuming any responsibility for what occurred. This event reveals a trait of his character, which is particularly uncongenial to the ideals of manliness of the Nordic races. He lacks the courage to defend an opinion openly, revealing a certain tendency to dodge and take advantage of subterfuges, to avoid an open espousal of his position."[70]

---

69 William Muir, Rede Lecture, delivered at Cambridge in 1881: *Asia, second edition*, revised and corrected. Published 1909, by E. Stanford in London, 458.

70 Tor Andrae, *Mohammed: The Man and His Faith* (Mineola, NY: Dover Publications, 1936, 2000), 145.

The Nakha raid also reveals the prophet's dishonesty, greed, and lack of loyalty to the adherents who were simply following his command. Muhammad was an accomplice to the entire devious plot, in which he broke three of the Ten Commandments: "You shall not murder. . . . You shall not steal. . . . You shall not bear false witness" (Exodus 20:13, 15, 16 NKJV).

Whenever the prophet needed to make an adjustment in the attitude of those around him, he would suddenly receive a "revelation"—at times, also, that seemed to provide for his own personal gain. In Sura 33:4, the prophet reveals Allah's somewhat unusual command to keep people from bothering him:

> O Believers! Enter not into the houses of the Prophet, save by his leave, for a meal, without waiting his time. When ye are invited then enter, and when ye have eaten then disperse at once. And engage not in familiar talk, for this would cause the Prophet trouble, and he would be ashamed to bid you go; but God is not ashamed to say the truth. And when ye would ask any gift of his wives, ask it from behind the veil. Purer will this be for your hearts and for their hearts. And ye must not trouble the Apostle of God.

Another example of the prophet's manipulations can be found in his relationship with his adopted son, Zaid, and Zaid's wife, Zainab, Muhammad's daughter-in-law. Muhammad was only six years older than Zaid, and he found Zainab to be quite beautiful. He made advances toward her, which began to arouse her ambition to become one of the wives of the prophet. Zaid felt inferior to his stepfather, and he could not handle Zainab's continual comparison of his lack to Muhammad's greatness. Zaid finally approached Muhammad and gave him permission to take Zainab as his wife. Muhammad refused, because he understood the scandal that would result—at first. Then he coincidentally received the "revelation" of Sura 33:37, which stated that it was Allah's will for Zainab to be given to Muhammad as his wife. And so it was that Zainab divorced Zaid and then married Muhammad.

As Muhammad rose to greater power, his harem of women also expanded. He had at least sixteen wives, two slaves, and four mis-

73

tresses. One of the slaves, Mary, was a Christian; because she refused to marry the prophet, she therefore remained a slave in his household. One of Muhammad's wives was only eight or nine years old when Muhammad married her—and took her to bed. He did all of these things in direct violation to his own revelation from Allah that allowed a man to marry no more than four women (Sura 4:3).

The prophet became a warrior for his own advancement. At the battle of Uhud, he was known for killing an enemy with his own hands. Greed was lavishly displayed in the large amount of riches and goods he amassed from raids on innocent towns and caravans. Those who opposed his religious views began to end up dead. All three of the Jewish tribes he had come to lead in Medina became objects of his wrath. Two of the tribes were forced to give him all of their possessions and then leave town. In fear that the other Jewish tribe in the city would cause him problems, he allowed a vengeful Arab who hated the Jews to have his wish. The Jewish men were all beheaded, and the women and children of their tribe were sold into slavery.

The Hadith, another "holy book" of Islam, reveals more about Muhammad's character in a collection of thousands of traditions and stories passed down from his life and from incidents that occurred during that time in history. Here are some interesting facts we can learn about Muhammad from the Hadith:

- Vol. 6, no. 435: Muhammad owned black slaves.
- Vol. 1, no. 90–91: Muhammad was short-tempered.
- Vol. 2, no. 555; Vol. 3, no. 391: Muhammad did not like anyone to question his claims of being a prophet or the validity of his revelations: "Allah has hated you . . . [for] asking too many questions." Vol. 1, no. 30 also tells us: "The Prophet told them repeatedly [in anger] to ask him anything they liked." But the people had learned not to ask him anything.
- Vol. 7, no. 636: Muhammad was extremely superstitious.[71]

71 Dr. Muhammad Muhsin Khan, *The Translation of the Meaning of Sahih Al-Bukhari* (Kazi Publications, Lahore, Pakistan, 1979), as recorded in Morey, 178–190.

Other Hadithic and Koranic sources expose Muhammad's lack of a sense of humor, his sexual appetites, and his bitterness and hatred toward those who did not support his prophetic claims. He had Abdulla bin Ubai bin Salul killed when the man mistakenly accused Aisha, one of Muhammad's wives, of adultery. And when Muhammad "peacefully" invaded Mecca—supposedly without bloodshed—he had certain people killed, especially those who had written poems or songs that ridiculed him.

Mixed Manifestations

Muhammad might have fallen victim to the selfishness that is a part of man's fallen nature, but in a rough land full of division, chaos, idolatry, and bloodshed, he still managed to bring a huge number of people into a unified force. He created a new and forceful world religion. This suggests he did have a noble desire to see his people become victorious. We can see in the life of Muhammad the long-ago prophecy of Ishmael, his ancestor, and the fallen nature that Cain exemplified, demonstrated in his actions and attitudes.

> "He shall be a wild man;His hand shall be against every man,
> And every man's hand against him.
> And he shall dwell in the presence of a
> ll his brethren." —Genesis 16:12 NKJV

We can only assume that Muhammad was convinced that his calling was, indeed, truly from God Himself. Yet Muhammad the man did not embody virtues that would clearly connect him with the God of the Bible. He was manipulative, dishonest, greedy, covetous, self-seeking, violent, and a murderer. This mixture of personality traits is what ultimately gave birth to the modern-day religion of Islam—and this spirit of a "wild warrior" seems to have been passed down from Muhammad to many of his descendants even to this day. In our modern era, we can see the same use of manipulation, treachery, deceit, and all manners of wicked "terrorist" tactics used to wreak havoc and force the religion of Islam on the lives of others.

The Lasting Consequences of a "Wild Warrior" Spirit

A former Muslim and professor of Islamic history at Al-Azhar University in Cairo, Egypt, author Mark Gabriel reminds us in his book *Islam and Terrorism* that: "Muhammad was born into a culture where conquest and bloodshed were the norm," and that "the majority of the Arabs entered Islam so that they would be rewarded with the possessions of people who would not submit to Islam." He also points out that a strong characteristic of the Arabs in the days of Muhammad was an "extremist mentality," which first became incorporated into the ideology of Islam and then eventually impacted the future adherents of the religion in other cultures and nations, such as Iran, Afghanistan, Pakistan, India, and elsewhere.[72]

The extreme fundamentalist attitude of Muhammad accompanied the religion of Islam wherever it marched, and it is still impacting cultures and nations today. At its founding, Islam set out to conquer all the nations and cultures of the world that were opposed to it—and that idea still exists today. For instance, one of the leading modern proponents of this ideology is Mawlana Abul Ala Mawdudi, the founder of Pakistan's fundamentalist movement. He explains his view of Islam in modern society as follows:

> Islam is a revolutionary faith that comes to destroy any government made by man. Islam doesn't look for a nation to be in better condition than another nation. Islam doesn't care about land or who owns the land. The goal of Islam is to rule the entire world and submit all of mankind to the faith of Islam. Any nation or power in this world that tries to get in the way of that goal, Islam will fight and destroy. In order for Islam to fulfill that goal, Islam can use every power available, every way it can be used, to bring worldwide revolution. This is jihad.[73]

---

72 Mark A. Gabriel, *Islam and Terrorism: Revised and Updated Edition* (Lake Mary, FL: Charisma Media/Charisma House Book Group, 2015), 62–63.
73 Syed Abul A'la Maududi, *Jihad in Islam*, second printing (Delhi 110006, India: Markazi Maktaba Islami, 1973).

Timeline 2: The Spread of Islam

CE 637–38: Muslims capture Jerusalem and many other cities.

661: Ali, Muhammad's nephew and the fourth caliph, is murdered, causing the Sunni-Shiite division that exists to this day.661–750: The Umayyad Muslim Dynasty begins. Mu'awiya sets up his capital in Damascus.

691: The construction of the Dome of the Rock is completed in Jerusalem.

700–717: Muslim armies conquer most of North Africa and Spain.

732: Charles Martel defeats the Muslims in southern France.

750–935: The Abbasid Dynasty begins when Mansur II is overthrown. The capital of Islam moves from Baghdad to Samaria, thus beginning the Golden Age of Islam.[74]

800–850: Sufism begins.[75]

846: The Muslims sack Rome.

874–999: A Sunni Iranian dynasty, the Samanids, rules from their capital in Bukhara.

900: The writing of *1001 Arabian Nights* begins, filled with chivalric romances, fairy tales, legends, fables, and other anecdotes.

909–972: The Shiite Fatimids set up a caliphate capital in Cairo, claiming ancestry to Muhammad's daughter, Fatima.

925: Cordoba, Spain, establishes another caliphate through the descendants of the Umayyad family.990–1118: The Seljūk Turkish family converts to Islam. Their war efforts spread the Islamic empire.1006: Muslims settle in India.

1094: El Cid defeats the Muslims in Spain.

1095: Pope Urban II calls for a crusade against the invading Turks.

---

74 Armstrong, 55.

75 Mojdeh Bayat and Mohammad Ali Jamnia, *Tales from the Land of the Sufis* (Boston, MA: Shambhala Publications, Inc., 2001), 10.

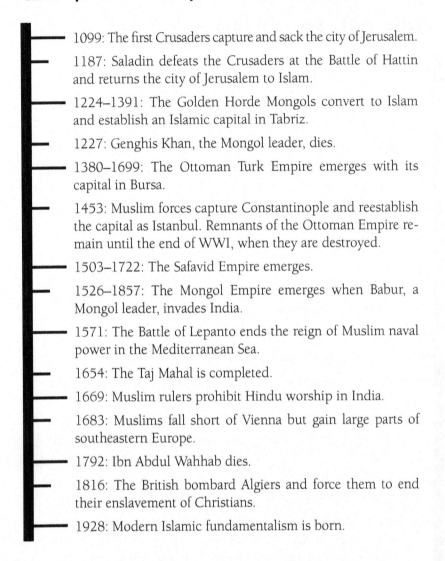

1099: The first Crusaders capture and sack the city of Jerusalem.

1187: Saladin defeats the Crusaders at the Battle of Hattin and returns the city of Jerusalem to Islam.

1224–1391: The Golden Horde Mongols convert to Islam and establish an Islamic capital in Tabriz.

1227: Genghis Khan, the Mongol leader, dies.

1380–1699: The Ottoman Turk Empire emerges with its capital in Bursa.

1453: Muslim forces capture Constantinople and reestablish the capital as Istanbul. Remnants of the Ottoman Empire remain until the end of WWI, when they are destroyed.

1503–1722: The Safavid Empire emerges.

1526–1857: The Mongol Empire emerges when Babur, a Mongol leader, invades India.

1571: The Battle of Lepanto ends the reign of Muslim naval power in the Mediterranean Sea.

1654: The Taj Mahal is completed.

1669: Muslim rulers prohibit Hindu worship in India.

1683: Muslims fall short of Vienna but gain large parts of southeastern Europe.

1792: Ibn Abdul Wahhab dies.

1816: The British bombard Algiers and force them to end their enslavement of Christians.

1928: Modern Islamic fundamentalism is born.

CHAPTER 5

The History of Islam

Islam was not a torch, as has been claimed, but an extinguisher. Conceived in a barbarous brain for the use of a barbarous people, it was —and it remains—incapable of adapting itself to civilization. Wherever it has dominated, it has broken the impulse towards progress and checked the evolution of society.[76]

—Andre Servier

Muhammad's Kind of Peace

People often recast the history of Muhammad and Islam in a sympathetic light, one that does not include the warring or domineering spirit that was manifested in the life of the prophet. For example, one historian said of Muhammad, "His surrender to God had been so complete that he had transformed society and enabled the Arabs to live together in harmony. The word *islam* is etymologically related to *salaam* (peace), and in these early years, Islam did promote cohesion and concord."[77]

Whatever "peace" Muhammad gained, however, it certainly wasn't peace for the Jews, who were driven from their homes during his reign in Medina, or for those who were slaughtered by his sword.

---

76 Andre Servier, *L'islam et la psychologie du musulman* (London: Chapman Hall LTD, 1924), 153.
77 Armstrong, 24.

After he conquered Mecca, it is true that large numbers of Arab tribes sent emissaries to him and accepted his religion of Islam, but it is equally true that "others submitted only after military pressure."[78] It was also true that he forced those who would not become Muslims to submit to Islamic law and to pay taxes that Muslims did not have to pay. This was subtle coercion, even though the Koran would later forbid coercion in matters of faith (Sutra 2:256). The South Arabian Christians of Nejran not only submitted, but they had to pay a tribute of two thousand garments, each worth at least an ounce of silver, in order to enjoy the prophet's "protection."[79]

Muhammad was a charismatic individual, but he constantly struggled with those around him. As it went with Ishmael, so Muhammad's hand was against every man's hand, and every man's hand was against his. When he died, about two years after his conquering of Mecca, peace had not yet been truly achieved. The wild spirit lived on in new militant leaders of the religion of Islam.

The First Four Caliphs

Muhammad had no sons. Neither did he appoint any successors, though some held that he had appointed Ali, his cousin and son-in-law, to take over upon his death. After the prophet's death, however, his closest followers met together and elected Abu Bakr (CE 632–634) as the new caliph. Abu Bakr was one of the first converts to Islam and the father of Aisha, the most beloved wife of Muhammad. His brief reign after Muhammad's death consisted largely of combat, mainly against those Arab tribes that had decided to turn against Islam upon the prophet's death. These conflicts became known as the Ridda Wars, or the Wars of Apostasy. Of the first four caliphs during that time, three were assassinated, and all were involved in warfare and the aggressive expansion of Islam.

Upon his deathbed, Abu Bakr did not give the community the chance to elect a successor. Instead, he himself nominated Umar (634–644), who also spent his caliphate in warfare. Umar conquered Damascus, Alexandria, Isfahan, and Jerusalem in 638 when

---

78 Andrae, 169.
79 Ibid., 170.

the Christian ruler Sophronius surrendered.[80] Author Ruqaiyyah Maqsood pointed out the Islamic polemic approach in his book, *Teach Yourself Islam*: "The formula was 'Islam, tribute, or sword,' the sword being reserved for those who refused to cooperate and pay the appropriate taxes. Those who did convert to Islam lived tax-free."[81] In 644, however, Umar was assassinated by a disgruntled non-Muslim.[82]

The committee then chose Uthman (644–656) as the third caliph to follow Muhammad. During his reign, the growing Muslim empire spread west across North Africa, and then east to the border of China and the Indus Valley. Uthman gained a bad reputation for promoting his own relatives to positions of power, and he ultimately died at the hand of the Egyptians. His wife, Nailah, tried to protect him, but her fingers were actually cut off in the fight. She sent her dismembered appendages, along with a plea for help, to Uthman's cousin, Mu'awiya, the governor of Damascus, in Syria.[83]

The split between what would eventually become known as the divide between Sunni and Shia Muslims began to emerge just twenty-four years after Muhammad's death (656–661), when Ali, Muhammad's cousin and son-in-law, finally staked a claim to be the rightful successor of the prophet. Aisha opposed his nomination. She declared that he was lax in justice and that he did not try to seek out those who had assassinated Uthman. Aisha led her own army against Ali, beginning the first of several civil wars. She was eventually captured at the Battle of Camel in 656, and was released to her friends in Madinah.

Also opposing Ali was Mu'âwiya, the governor at Damascus. His reasoning was also that Ali had not gone after the murderers of Uthman. Through his negligence, it appeared as though Ali had tacitly supported the assassins. In 661, Mu'âwiya's army was strong in Arabia. Because Ali began to fear defeat, he finally agreed to an election between himself and Mu'âwiya. However, this move greatly

---

80 Cooper, 210.
81 Ruqaiyyah Maqsood, *Teach Yourself Islam* (Lincolnwood, IL: NTC/Contemporary Publishing, 1994), 22.
82 Ibid., 163.
83 Maqsood, 23.

offended some of Ali's own warriors, because they believed he was the rightful caliph and that an election should not take place. These warriors then seceded from his ranks and created the Khârijites, or Seceders. This group later assassinated Ali while he was praying.

Within just two decades following Muhammad's death, the Islamic armies had conquered vast swaths of land, from northern Africa to the Caucasus, and in the east beyond Iran to the Oxus River in present-day Afghanistan.[84] The rewards were plentiful. The once-disunited bands of nomads who had occasionally plundered a caravan now and again, had become a united horde of self-seeking, greedy, "early Islamic fundamentalists." All for the "glory of Allah," the more they spread the faith of Islam, the more riches they gained by conquering and looting both villages and nations. The revenues from the lands they conquered were used to provide pensions for the descendants of Muhammad.[85]

Behind the fury of the Islamic storm that was rapidly spreading, a great schism was forming that would ultimately fracture the heart of the teachings and of the people. The genuine adherents of the faith became dismayed, because the "noble side" of Islamic teaching—including equality, unity, community, service to Allah, and the spreading of the message—were being overshadowed by the baser elements of human greed, power, lust, debauchery, and cruelty. Sin seemed to always be crouching at the door.

The Umayyad Dynasty (CE 661–750)

The initial purpose of the Islamic caliphate was to serve the cause and to spread the message of Islam. In reality, however, the caliphate ended up serving the purposes of a small group of rich, powerful men who essentially ruled by tyranny. When Mu'âwiya took control in CE 661, Islam took another step toward empowering a centralized autocracy, which continued to drain the influence of the Islamic community. In his book *Islam in History*, Bernard Lewis points out the dilemma:

---

84 Weiss, 19.
85 Ibid., 20.

By a tragic paradox, only the strengthening of the Islamic state could save the identity and cohesion of the Islamic community—and the Islamic state, as it grew stronger, moved further away from the social and ethical ideas of Islam. Resistance to this process of change was constant and vigorous, sometimes successful, but always unavailing—and out of this resistance emerged a series of religious sects, different in their ideologies and their support but alike in seeking to restore the radical dynamism that was being lost.[86]

As mentioned previously, when Ali, Muhammad's relative, attempted to make himself the successor of Muhammad, two major sects began to emerge within Islam: the Sunni and the Shiites. The Sunni followed the caliphate, but the Shiites looked to the descendants of Ali as their spiritual leaders. This division caused more bloodshed and war within Islam.

Throughout the ninety years of the Umayyad Dynasty, the Islamic armies conquered all of North Africa, as well as the country of Spain. Spain would remain under Islamic rule for seven hundred years, until the terrible Spanish Inquisition expelled Islam in 1492.

The Dome of the Rock was completed at the Temple site in Jerusalem in CE 691. It was the first major Islamic monument to be constructed, and its completion reinforced to the Christians—the majority religion—the idea that Islam was there to stay.[87] However, the defeat of the eighty thousand Muslim warriors in southern Europe by Charles Martel's army of just thirty thousand troops in CE 732 sent the Umayyad army into full retreat, thus slowing their advances westward.

Within Islam, Shiite revolutions became just one source of agitation. Converts to Islam, called *mawalis* (or, "clients"), had become resentful, second-class citizens. If they weren't Arabs, the differences were even greater. Also, Islam was becoming more and more hostile toward Christians and any people of other faiths. By CE 705, the Church of Saint John at Damascus, which had been shared for both

---

86 Bernard Lewis, *Islam in History: Ideas, People, and Events in the Middle East* (Peru, IL: Open Court Publishing Company, 2001), 296–297.
87 Armstrong, 44.

Muslim and Christian worship, was completely taken over by the Muslims, and the Arabic language began to replace the traditional Greek language that had been spoken there for centuries.[88]

The Abbasid Dynasty (CE 750–935)

The Abbasid faction capitalized on a widespread desire to see a descendant of Muhammad leading the new religion of Islam. In 750, the last Umayyad caliph, Mansur II, was defeated in Iraq. The new leader would be Abdallah, a direct descendant of the prophet's uncle Abbas.[89]

With the advent of the new dynasty, some things in Islamic society improved, while others got worse. The traditional privileges of birth and race gradually gave way to more equal opportunities for all Muslims, not just Arab-Muslims. Commerce and the marketplace grew in both productivity and status. The streets of Baghdad—the new capital of the dynasty—bustled with business activity.

The Abbasid Dynasty seemed peaceful for a while, but then it began to deteriorate into persecution and warfare. According to author Bernard Lewis, the Umayyad Arab aristocrats were replaced by the "bureaucratic Abbasid state, with its well-ordered civil service and its professional army." Outwardly, they displayed all the trappings of Islamic piety, but inwardly they were far more distant from Islamic ideals. Government became more complex and more oppressive—especially toward Christians living under their rule.[90] Author Anne Cooper writes: "History records the forcible conversion of the 'last Christian tribe in Syria', the Banu Tanukh."[91] The Christians had been resisting Islam for many years, and they had often received help from the Byzantine emperor, but on the order of the caliph al-Madhi (775–785), they now were required to become Muslims.

Muslims were constantly invading, conquering, and ransacking various communities outside of their own borders. In CE 856 the Muslims sacked Rome and the Vatican. Although they could not

---

88 Cooper, 211.
89 Armstrong, 53.
90 Lewis, 309–310.
91 Cooper, 217.

successfully maintain any foothold in that part of Europe for any length of time, there were continual war parties scouting around to confiscate more wealth, goods, and land. During the Abbasid Dynasty, the Muslims did gain control of northern India, along with the area down to the Bay of Bengal.[92]

Within Islamic society, there was always the danger that some fanatic might invoke the Sharia (Islamic law) as an excuse for destroying Christian churches. The caliph Harun-al Rashid ordered all Christians and Jews to wear distinctive clothing. This policy was fully in force by CE 807. Later, Muhammad's grandson al-Mutawakkil restored these orders and added even further decrees designed to humiliate the Christians under Islamic rule.

Near the end of the dynasty, changes were taking place across Islam. A Persian named Husayn Ibn Mansur Hallaj became a Sufi master and proclaimed that he—like Jesus Christ—was the "truth" and that he needed to be martyred to atone for people's sin. Hallaj got his wish when he was blamed for a series of revolts and coups that

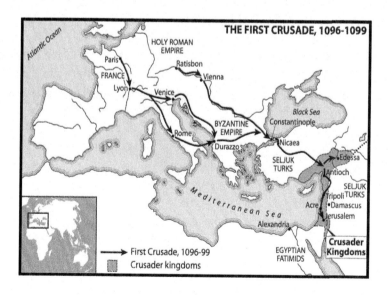

---

92 John R. Hinnells, ed., *A Handbook of Living Religions* (New York, NY: Penguin Books, 1987), 129.

broke out in Baghdad, and he was brutally executed.[93] Sufism, a mystical Islamic sect, began to grow as a result after that incident.

The Golden Age of Islam

The Abbasid Dynasty also ushered in an advancement of science, medicine, mathematics, philosophy, and literature, so much so that this time period became known as the Golden Age of Islam. This was the era of the writing of the *1001 Arabian Nights*, which was ultimately a collection of numerous literary styles. Also written during this time frame was Al Sufi's *Book of Fixed Stars*, which mentioned the astronomical concept of the nebula. In CE 900, the Arab physician Rhases became the first to describe smallpox, the plague, and other infectious diseases. Later, in the eleventh century, Avicenna (Ibn Sina) became the most influential Islamic medieval philosopher in history.

The Golden Age of Islam was truly remarkable, and it brought advancements in many scientific and philosophical arenas. However, it is important for every student of history to recognize that these advancements did not happen without outside help—from those who were not part of the state of Islam. Both Christian and Jewish scholars played a major role in what is called the "formative period," that is, the period of time just before the Golden Age. Consider the following regarding some of the contributions made by Christian scholars:

> Already in late antiquity, Hellenistic philosophy found its way into Semitic language: not Arabic, but Syriac. In a foreshadowing of the 'Abbasid-sponsored-Greek-Arabic translations, Christian scholars working at monasteries in Syria produced versions of works by Aristotle and other Greek thinkers. Some Christians, for instance Sergius of Resh'ayna (d. 536), composed their own philosophical treatises. This Christian scholarly tradition provided continuity between the Hellenistic and Islamic cultures. When Islam spread through the Near East, Greek-speaking Christians fell within its sphere of influence. They retained their religious beliefs,

---

93 Bayat and Jamnia, 19–20.

and there continued to be scholars with facility in both Greek and Syriac. So when the 'Abbasid caliphs and other wealthy patrons of the eighth through tenth centuries decided to have Greek scientific works rendered into Arabic, most of the translators they hired were Christians. This activity was centered in Iraq and particularly Baghdad, the new capital city founded by the early 'Abbasid caliph al-Mansur.[94]

Some believe that during the Golden Age of Moorish Spain, Muslims, Christians, and Jews lived in harmony within a tolerant, enlightened, and upwardly mobile Islamic culture. Conversely, however, it was the fragmentation of that society and the jihadist spirit that spurred on the crusading *Reconquesta*, the reconquering of Spain by the Christians.[95]

Convivencia was a Spanish term that meant "living together." When applied to religion, it would delineate the concept of Christian, Jew, and Muslim living together in mutual respect for each other's benefit. The term *Mozarabs* referred to Christians living under Moorish rule, and *Mudejar* was vice versa. Spanish historians suggest that during the Golden Age of Moorish Spain, there were experiments in *convivencia*, producing many harmonious and intellectual relationships.[96]

Intellectual sharing took place during this time. Spain, as well as other countries that were influenced by the Golden Age, produced Muslim philosophers such as Averroes and Avicenna; Maslama, the astronomer; Jewish poets like Yehuda HaLevi; Jewish scholars like Maimonides; etc. Eleventh-century Cordoba boasted a library of four hundred thousand books. At the university in Toledo, Jews, Arabs, and Greeks all cooperated with Spaniards, Italians, and Englishmen to translate books of philosophy, science, medicine, and

94 Peter Adamson, *Philosophy in the Islamic World: A Very Short Introduction* (Oxford, England: Oxford University Press, 2015), 7-9.
95 *Columbia Encyclopedia,* Sixth Edition, "Pelayo," (Columbia University Press, 2001).
96 Richard Fletcher, *Moorish Spain* (Los Angeles, CA: University of California Press, 1992), 134.

other great scholastic works.[97] Translations of works by Aristotle and other great thinkers would then stimulate future intellectualism in Europe. Also, Christians and Jews were allowed to maintain a limited self-government.

Yet Moorish Spain was not always so "golden," and other cultures were not so uncivilized. The tradition and process of translating important books actually began in southern Italy, not Spain.[98] Peaceful relationships between Christians, Muslims, and Jews were promoted in Norman, Sicily, as well as in the Christian principalities in the crusader states of Syria and Palestine.[99] In fact, one Islamic traveler, Ibn Jubayr, visited Tibnin, near Tyre, and expressed frustration because the Muslim inhabitants who lived with the Franks actually lived in comfort and were treated with equity, but Muslims who dealt only with one another suffered injustices.[100]

Convivencia was not always harmonious, however. Some rightly suggest that the Golden Age, in regard to equal rights, was simply a myth.[101] The Mozarabs of Al Andalus, just like the Copts of Egypt, were treated as second-class citizens and often lived in demoralizing conditions.[102] Insurrections and wars were not uncommon among these people.

The "goldenness of tolerance" was also suspect during this time. Numerous Christian martyrs were reported in ninth-century Cordoba; persecutions of Almazor and Abd al-Malik blazed against Christians in the tenth century; the Jews of Granada were massacred in the eleventh century (CE 1066); and numerous Christians were deported to Morocco in the twelfth century (CE 1126).

The goldenness of learning was also stifled. Scholarship was limited to a small percentage, for those in the circles of princely

---

97 Christopher Dawson, *Religion and the Rise of Western Culture*, Image Books edition (New York: Doubleday, 1991), 191–192. Dawson suggests that Toledo, for a time, became similar to the universities that were flourishing in Paris and Bologna.
98 Ibid.
99 Fletcher, 135.
100 Amin Maalouf, *The Crusades Through Arab Eyes* (New York: Schocken Books, Inc., 1984), 263.
101 Bernard Lewis, *Peace Encyclopedia*, Mitchell Bard, referencing Bernard Lewis, "The Pro-Islam Jews," *Judaism* (Fall 1968), 401.
102 Fletcher, 173.

courts.[103] Jews and Mozarabs were prohibited from flourishing, and the latter lost any intellectual initiative.[104] Yehuda was a Zionist who was reacting to restrictions in Moorish society, including clothing identification for Jews. His poems yearned for Jerusalem.[105] Also, Maimonides's family fled from Cordoba to Morocco, Palestine, and then Cairo because of religious persecution.

The image of *convivencia* is appealing, but not compelling. Source evidence does not ever demonstrate the reality of a harmonious, long-lasting, tolerant, and equitable *convivencia*. Probably, like any other forced coexistence, there were ups and downs in relationships. The "Reconquest" began in 718 by Pelayo and continued to emerge throughout the centuries. In the tenth century, during the Moorish *Dar*-Djihad—the land of jihad—Christian Leon, Castile, and other kingdoms started numerous battles with a crusading spirit, in order to take back Al Andalus. In 1236, Cordoba fell to Christians, but the city had been in a state of decline for many centuries at the Muslim's own hands, through conspiracy, assassination, slave revolts, and insurrection.[106] Century by century, the battles continued, until the Reconquest was finally complete in 1492.[107]

Causes of the Original Crusading Spirit

The military expansion of Islam sparked the crusading spirit in Christian feudal states that had been created by war and for war.[108] Islam's progressive conquest over the centuries and its internal rivalries invaded the physical security of Europe, fashioned spiritual alarm about the Holy Land, and drew forth armed retaliation. A crusading spirit arose among Christians against the spirit of militant jihad.

---

103 Ibid., 172.
104 Library of Congress Country Studies, "Spain, Al Andalus" (December 1998).
105 Lindsay Faber, "A Zionist in Andalusia's golden age," *U.S. News & World Report*, 127 (August 16–23, 1999), no. 750.
106 Joel L. Swerdlow, "Alexandria, Cordoba, and New York: A Tale of Three Cities," *National Geographic* (August 1999), 196, No. 2.
107 *Si, Spain*, "The Reconquest" (May 1994); www.sispain.org/english/history/reconque.html.
108 Dawson, 140.

Within two decades after Muhammad's death in CE 632, the Muslims had conquered land from northern Africa to the Caucasus, and in the east beyond modern Iran to the Oxus River in Afghanistan. Arab Islamic armies caught cities off-guard and unprepared, cities that had experienced a measure of peace since the end of the wars between the Christian Byzantine and Zoroastrian Persian empires.

The death toll of Christian Palestine finally sounded in February 638, when the patriarch Sophronius was forced to surrender Jerusalem to the Muslims. It was reported that shortly afterward, he died of a "broken heart."[109] The early Islamic formula for conquering Jerusalem, as elsewhere, was to the point: convert to Islam, pay a tribute, or meet the sword—the sword primarily reserved for those who refused to cooperate or to pay taxes. Converts would live tax-free.[110] The worldview of Islam gave outsiders a poignant caution: Everything that took place within Islam was part of the *House of Islam*, or the *House of Peace* (*dar-al Islam*), but everything outside of that was the *House of War* (*dar-al Harb*).

The political and religious unity of Islam did not survive the rule of the first four warring caliphs. A concentric, Arab-dominated Islam dissolved, as conquered communities converted, adding their character and culture to the spread and leadership of Islam. The power base shifted under the Umayyad Dynasty (661–750) to Damascus, and then in the Abbasid Dynasty (750–935) to Baghdad and Samarra.[111] Within Islam, doctrinal schisms about Muhammad's lineage and how Islam was to be ruled split radical Shiites from orthodox Sunnis. Eventually, Sufi mysticism created even more schisms. By 925, during the Abbasid Dynasty, there were also power bases emerging in the Iranian Sunni capital of Bukhara, in the Egyptian Shiite capital of Cairo, and in an emerging caliphate in Cordoba, Spain. When the Seljûk Turks rose to power, defeating the eastern Byzantines at Manzikert and then capturing Jerusalem in 1071, it brought special alarm to the Christian West.[112]

---

109 Steven Runciman, *The First Crusade—Canto Edition* (New York: Cambridge University Press, 1992), 2.
110 Maqsood, 22.
111 Armstrong, 63.
112 Runciman, 27–29.

There was also a spiritual concern. Before the Turkish invasion, Christian pilgrims had been allowed access to the holy sites in Palestine—but now this access was intermittent or often denied altogether, and pilgrims were randomly robbed and/or murdered while visiting the Holy Land.

Before the Middle Ages, Christendom had no well-defined concept of "holy war," as Islam did.[113] Christianity had preached a peace not yet achieved.[114] Christian Rome's central control destabilized as it dealt with paganism and further invasions by barbarians. These wars obliterated any hope of pacific development and produced feudal Christian states with a warrior ethos.[115] By the tenth century, there was an emergence of French chivalry and the belief that the "Christian knight who died in battle for the faith" was both hero and martyr.[116]

The warring efforts of Emperor Charlemagne and his son, Pepin, in the ninth century possibly foreshadowed the Crusades, as did the rising resistance in Spain. After conquering the Berbers (or, barbarians) in the area of northwest Africa called the Maghrib, Arabic Islam strategically employed converted Berbers in CE 711 to attack the Visigoths in Al Andalus (ancient Spain). By CE 715, they had taken the entire Iberian Peninsula, and their conquest continued on to Gaul, Toulouse, and Burgundy, but the Muslims were checked and driven back at Poitiers in CE 732 by Charles Martel.

Yet even before Martel's victory, a symbolic battle occurred sometime prior, between CE 718 and 725, at Covadonga in northern Spain. A small Christian army, led by Visigothic king Pelayo, imposed the first defeat on the Muslims. Supposedly this marked the beginning of the *Reconquesta*, or the reconquering of Spain by the Christians. But the Reconquest would take hundreds of years to achieve, during which time Moorish Spain supposedly enjoyed

---

113 Thonas Madden, *A Concise History of the Crusades* (Oxford, England: Rowman & Littlefield Publishers, Inc., 1999), 1.
114 Runciman, 7.
115 Dawson suggests that the Christian wars with barbarians almost destroyed Christianity, and thus they were more of a crusade than even the formal Crusades themselves, 87–88.
116 Dawson, 142, 146.

its Golden Age, taking leadership over from Western culture in the tenth century.[117]

However, tenth-century Spain was also known colloquially as the *Dar*-Djihad, or "the land of jihad."[118] For instance, there was a great slaughter of Christians at Valdejunquera in CE 920 by Córdoban armies. In the late tenth and early eleventh centuries, the ruler Almazor and his son, Abd al-Malik, launched continual battles northward into the Christian principalities, sacking cities, persecuting Christians, and destroying entire communities.

There is a certain line of reasoning that has been around since the time of the rise of Islam, which holds that Islam represents the fifth trumpet found in the book of Revelation, chapter 9. The Islamic marauders on horses, with long hair and yellow turbans, holding banners of the crescent moon, could possibly represent the images of "crowns of something like gold," "women's hair," and "tails like scorpions" found in this biblical passage (see Revelation 9:7–10 NKJV).

In Europe, by the end of the eleventh century, eastern and western Christendom had diverged both politically and ecclesiastically. Constantinople ruled the East, and Rome the West. Within the West, there were warring feudal states, heretical issues, and criminal activities. Also, there was ongoing encroachment by Islam at its borders. The conquests of the Córdoban armies in Spain and the Seljûk Turks in the Christian Byzantine East created insecurity and birthed an even greater resentment of Islam's hold over the ancient holy sites in Palestine. The spirit of the Crusades had been ignited in the West.

The Crusades

The word *crusade* is modern. It is derived from the medieval word *crucesignati*, meaning "those signed by the cross." Modern use of the word *crusade* has developed various meanings and now the word does not necessarily convey the religious inference of *crucesignati*—yet the spirit of passion can still be ignited by worthy causes in each of us.

---

117 Ibid., 84–85.
118 Fletcher, 61.

When Pope Urban II made his speech at the Council of Clermont in 1095, it ignited passion for the first Crusade. The exact wording has been lost to history. However, chronicler Robert the Monk reports of specific atrocities having been committed against Christians in the East by the Turks.[119] Fulcher of Chartres tells of the pope's two basic driving points in his speech, being inner cleansing and the need for a military response to help the Christians in the East.[120] Jerusalem should be rescued from the Muslim infidels—and this could happen only if Christians in the West would quit squabbling with each other and begin to unite themselves against Islam. For those who died along the way or in battle, the pope offered absolution and the remission of sins. This speech by Pope Urban II birthed a vision of a crusade that would change the future relationship between western Christendom and eastern Byzantine Christendom, as well as the Islamic world.

Life in the Middle Ages was not easy. There was a kind of *otherworldly* sense in a typical Christian's thinking, as well as an ignorance of the New Testament doctrine that prohibits violence (due to most people's illiteracy), so that the people unwittingly rose to the call of the pope. Within months, there might have been as many as 150,000 men, women, and children who took up the pilgrim vows. They had the sign of the cross as a symbol sewn onto their clothing. Then they set out on a two-thousand-mile journey to find "favor with Christ" by rescuing Jerusalem. Noblemen and knights joined the crusade due to a simple and sincere love for God, but the vast majority of the people who joined up were poor men and women, of whom many were elderly. The mixture of Christian virtue and barbarous war tactics made them pious, idealistic, and faithful, but also crude, arrogant, and savage at times.[121]

Unfortunately, the first Crusade was marked by disorganization, outbreaks against the Jews, shuffling for power among the nobles, and a terrible slaughter when they finally were able to conquer Je-

---

119 Madden, 8–9.
120 Paul Halsall, "Medieval Sourcebook: Urban II: Speech at Council of Clermont, 1095, according to Fulcher of Chartres" (March 1996).
121 Madden, 12.

rusalem. All in all, it was a bloody war, in which terrible things happened—yet the crusaders were victorious. There were some positive characteristics of this crusade that shone forth, including the very real sense of personal sacrifice, acts of kindness, chivalry, vision, faith, miracles, and a tenacity for accomplishing God's will. The crusade, in its purest form, was truly an act of selfless piety for the salvation of one's soul.[122] Of course, not all of the crusaders necessarily had what modern evangelicals would call a "personal salvation relationship" with the Lord Jesus Christ. Yet, in the theology of that day, the crusaders embraced this self-sacrifice in the holy cause of rescuing Jerusalem from the Muslims, and through this, they believed that they had truly earned an eternal reward.

Four years after the first Crusade began, the crusaders captured Jerusalem, but it eventually fell back into Muslim hands again, when Saladin defeated the crusaders at the Battle of Hattin in 1187. For almost two centuries, the Muslims and Christians fought over possession of the Holy Land. These conquests were some of the most aggressive military campaigns that Christians would ever employ against Muslims—and some of them were marked with great brutality.

When the crusading spirit arose as a necessary reaction to the spirit of militant jihad, it secured Western Christendom for a time, and it did successfully counteract the spread of Islam at that time. Without it, Seljûk Turks, Mamluks, Moors, Ottomans, and even Mongols could have stormed through Europe, and the demographics of the world that we know today would not exist. Christianity could very well have been extinguished by Islam, gone the way of Zoroastrianism.[123] Both Europe and the Americas would have been engulfed by Islam, and we would be facing a very different religious picture in our world today.

Within Islam, however, the doctrine of militant jihad reacted violently to anything that was in opposition to Koranic doctrine and

---

122 Madden discusses this in relationship to the betrayal of Frederick II, who appeared successful in the crusade of 1229, but it was done through secular means and without such spiritual passion, 164.
123 Thomas F. Madden, "The Real History of the Crusades," *Crisis* magazine (April 1 2002).

tradition. It had to be extinguished if peace was to have any chance. Its arrogant, irrational, and threatening manner was like a Goliath in the earth. A shepherd boy named David spoke up and said, "Is there not a cause" to fight (see 1 Samuel 17:29 NKJV)? And thus he slung the stone that slayed Goliath.

Cultural trends later altered the character and purpose of crusading, but the crusading spirit was, by then, a part of the Western Christian worldview. The spirit of passion and commitment of the first Crusade was to be carried on for generations by individuals such as St. Louis IX, king of France,[124] or groups like the misguided children in the children's crusades. However, contemporary movements determined a purpose be found in the crusade itself. For example, the Wendish Crusade's goal was not to drive out the infidel, but to convert them by the sword.[125] By the time of the Second Crusade, which was a failure, the *Reconquesta* in Spain was emerging. This expanded the definition of a *crusade* to also include fighting home-based wars in defense of the faith.[126]

The disastrous Fourth Crusade permanently split West and East Christendom when the Crusaders sacked Christian Constantinople in 1204. The Crusades now justified attacking Christians in opposition to the Crusaders' goals. *Political* crusades at home in Europe were now emerging, and the Fourth Crusade's change in its crusading concept now justified fighting heretics—not just Muslims, but also Christians who believed differently than the crusader. Thus was ignited the Albigensian Crusade of the thirteenth century in France, and eventually the Hussite Crusade of the fifteenth century in Bohemia. Ultimately, one motif of the crusade simply became: any war against the adversaries of the papal policy.[127] This could have eventually included any or all Protestants, if the respect for the papacy and the institution of Christian knighthood had not crumbled in the fifteenth century.[128]

---

124 Steven Runciman, *A History of the Crusades, Volume III: The Kingdom of Acre and the Later Crusades* (New York: Cambridge University Press, 1999), 258.
125 Madden, 58.
126 Ibid., 123.
127 Runciman, *A History of the Crusades*, 472.
128 Madden, 201, 209.

Although Pope Gregory X decided the crusading spirit was moribund[129] in the late thirteenth century, international crusades continued, until the Crusade of Nicropolis in 1397.[130] The fall of Constantinople in 1453 to the Muslims marked the end of Byzantine history.[131] Yet, the completion of the *Reconquesta* in 1492 and the immediate expansion of Spanish conquest into the New World mimicked the concept of the Crusades. The crusading spirit helped to spawn the idea of "manifest destiny" and the European westward movement, but then it diffused into numerous fragmented ideological meanings.

Today, the idea of "crusade" has changed. There are evangelistic crusades and other crusades for charities and political causes. Any type of reform conducted with zeal could be called a crusade. One professor lists four characteristics of modern movements that we could call crusades: 1) a moral cause based on Christian principles; 2) any long-term commitment to a cause by a minority group; 3) any victory achieved by suffering and struggle against enemies with a powerful belief system that opposes your own; and 4) a response to unexpected results.[132] So, the concept of "crusade" has survived, albeit in an altered form consistent with contemporary need. Maintaining a crusade mentality helps individuals or groups respond to causes.

Hindsight tells us that there were great mistakes made in the medieval Crusades fought between Christians and Muslims. Some of the Church's actions have brought great reproach on the name of our Prince of Peace, Jesus Christ. Yet, those who fought in them might disagree. The conflict did not develop in a vacuum or as a result of Christians being converted to Islam. Author Karen Armstrong observes that, even though the wars were devastating for the Muslims of the Near East, "the vast majority of Muslims in Iraq,

---

129 Runciman, *A History of the Crusades*, 401.

130 Ibid., 461.

131 Steven Runciman, *The Fall of Constantinople, 1453* (New York: Cambridge University Press, 2001), 189.

132 For a full definition, see William Urban, "Rethinking the Crusades," *Perspectives Online* (October 1998); historians.org.

Iran, Central Asia, Malaysia, Afghanistan, and India" only knew of them as remote border wars.[133] Also, another source states: "The Muslims, unlike the Christians, did not regard the Crusades as something separate and distinctive, nor did they single out the Crusaders from the long series of infidel [non-Muslim] enemies whom from time to time they fought."[134]

Before the Crusades ended, Christian missionaries, acting in the true character of the faith, went forth in peace to preach the Gospel. During the Fifth Crusade, Saint Francis of Assisi went out to share his faith with the sultan of Egypt. Later, in the same year, five Franciscan monks were martyred in Morocco. Within a hundred years, another missionary, Raymond Lull, took the Gospel message to Tunis, Africa, where he also was martyred.[135]

Early in the twentieth century, when the West began eclipsing the Islamic nations with military power, Islamic historians became preoccupied with the medieval Crusades, hoping for another Saladin to arise.[136] As a result, the Crusades have gradually become a modern justification for current irrational Islamic fundamental warfare. What seems to be ignored by historians who are sympathetic to Islam is the fact that Islamic warriors of the seventh and eighth centuries had first invaded all parts of Christendom and advanced into Spain, Portugal, southern Italy, and France, ordering the people of these Christian lands to either convert, pay an unreasonable amount of money, or die by the sword.

Still, during the 1990s, a movement occurred in which Christians began to travel to Europe and the Near East to walk the paths of the Crusaders in a series of "reconciliation walks." As they went forth, Christians asked forgiveness of the Muslims and the Jews for any historical atrocities that had taken place in the name of Jesus Christ. Many amazing testimonies surfaced from these walks, like those of my wife's aunt Linda, who went on two of them. She saw some

---

133 Armstrong, 95.
134 Lewis quoting Professor Gabrieli, 116–117.
135 Cooper, 214.
136 Armstrong, ibid.

Muslims rejoice and even weep in gladness that Christians were asking forgiveness for what had taken place in the ancient past. Others could not conceive why modern Christians felt the need to repent of past atrocities. But Linda had numerous opportunities to pray with Muslims for peace and for a clearer understanding of the truth.

The Great Islamic Empires of the Past

Historians indicate that a steady infusion of nomadic people from the Turkish steppe area gave Islam access to fresh leadership and greater military prowess. The continual conquest and advancement of Islam funneled its followers into combat with many types of people. The unspoiled virtues of new nomadic converts kept the corrupting influences of the empire in check.[137] The Turkish Seljûks, Egyptian Mamluks, Asian Mongols, and Anatolian Ottomans all brought fresh vitality for conquest and dominance.

Islam reached the land of Mongolia sometime in the first half of the thirteenth century, and it had a great impact.[138] Then Hulagu, the grandson of Mongol Chieftain Genghis Khan, invaded India in 1258 with his Mongol army of nomads, and he conquered everything in his path. The last Abbasid caliph fell to them in Baghdad. It wasn't until 1260 that the Mongols' advancement was stopped in Palestine.

The rise of the Ottoman, Safavid, and Mongol empires took the Islamic faith and its concept of state religions to new levels of strength and influence. The Ottoman Empire, which began in the thirteenth century in northwest Anatolia, conquered Syria, Iraq, the Balkans, Egypt, and the Red Sea area, and it laid siege to Vienna twice. In 1453, Mehmed II conquered the Christian bastion of Constantinople by using new weaponry armed with gunpowder. The city was renamed Istanbul, and it became the new capital. Further, they turned the St. Sophia Basilica into a mosque. The Ottoman Em-

---

137 Lewis analyzes Ibn Khaldun's thoughts. He was considered the greatest of Arab historians from the fourteenth century, 203. Cooper also emphasizes Ibn Khaldun's views of the Seljuks, Mamluks, Mongols, and Ottomans, as well as later historians who confirm his opinions, 168.

138 "Mongolia History," Wikipedia; https://en.wikipedia.org/wiki/Islam_in_Mongolia#History (accessed March 31, 2016).

pire remained strong until the Treaty of Karlowitz signed in 1699, but vestiges of the empire lasted all the way up until the end of World War I.

The Safavid (1503–1722) and Moghal empires (1526–1857) did not last as long as the Ottoman Empire, but each was important in establishing Islam in those areas. In the Safavid Empire, Shâh Abbas quenched the political feuding while successfully restructuring the institutions of the Islamic state. In the Moghal Empire, a Mongol army invaded India near Dehli and eventually took the entirety of southern India. Shâh Jehân built the majestic Taj Mahal in 1654 as a

The Three Muslim Empires

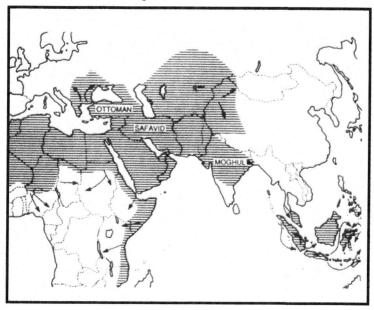

tomb for himself and his favorite wife. And as with the many previous examples, Islam once again showed its intolerance in 1669 by prohibiting Hindu worship in India. Later, in nineteenth-century Iran, thousands of adherents to the Baha'i cult were slaughtered simply for espousing their religious beliefs.

Over time, the evolving cultural and technological advances of the West gradually created a widening gulf between itself and the Islamic religious culture that preferred to hold on to the past. The weapons of the West soon controlled the battles. In 1571, the naval Battle of Nepanto ended any Islamic naval activities in the Mediterranean Sea. In 1816, the superior British armory bombarded Algiers and forced them to end the enslavement of Christians. European colonialism and dominance ultimately became inevitable. The Great Empires had fallen—their end had come.

PART THREE

TENETS OF THE FAITH

———— ✡ ✝ ☪ ————

CHAPTER 6

Rituals and Beliefs

Sadly, grace is often absent in Islam, which is based upon binding religious law, requiring strenuous adherence to every tenet of the "Five Pillars of Allah."... A religion that emerges from the soil of strict adherence to law as a means of gaining God's favor will always tend toward extreme self-sacrifice.[139]

—Carey Cash

The Five Pillars of Islam

In chapter 1, we considered various statistics of how dedicated Muslims are to follow the pillars of Islam. As with any religion, those who associate with Islam vary greatly in their devotion and in their method of devotion. There are those who follow all of the religious rites and those who do not.

For example, In sub-Saharan Africa, nine out of ten Muslims pray five times a day, but in other parts of Africa only four to six out of every ten do so. The Haj, the once-in-a-lifetime pilgrimage to Mecca explained below, is rarely practiced by adherents from any nation or region of the world, with the highest attendance being 17 percent of Muslims from the Middle East and the North Africa regions. Mosque attendance is high in many places, but it is as low

---

139 Tim Reid, "'Islam is violent' says President Obama's new pastor, Carey Cash," *The Times* (October 15, 2009), as recorded in "Quotations on Islam from Notable Non-Muslims"; wikiislam.net.

as three out of ten in Uzbekistan. Gender plays a role also. For instance, in Pakistan most men go to the mosque, but only half of the women attend.[140]

Below are listed the five basic pillars of Islam that drive Muslim life. The simplicity of these personal obligations has given this religion its growing appeal. Christians should understand all five of these pillars. Cultural sensitivity is critical for reaching the Muslims in the community—and around the world.

1. To Recite the *Shahadah*

The shortest religious creed in the world is the creed of Islam:

> There is no god but Allah and Muhammad is his messenger.

Obviously, repeating a phrase does not make it true, but it has been proven to be an effective means of brainwashing or mentally conditioning individuals. Devout Muslims recite this phrase constantly. The words, which are whispered into the ears of a newborn infant, are repeated throughout the child's life, and are often the last words spoken before death. The words are used for the call to prayer five times a day, and they are a comfort at times of crisis.[141] They are the mental foundation for Islamic life, spoken so often that they become ingrained into a person's thought and belief systems and challenge any alternative thinking.

The Shahadah is also used at conversion to the religion of Islam. According to Maqsood, when someone utters these words before two witnesses and truly believes the words in his heart, he has entered the Islamic faith. The proof can be seen in the individual's changed life and their adherence to the sharia, or Islamic law. The person must not eat pork or other forbidden animal products. They are also to give up alcohol, any entertainment based on the social aspects of alcohol, and immodest ways of dress. Furthermore, they are also to give up arrogance, selfishness, deceitfulness, and any other character weaknesses.[142]

---

140 "The World's Muslims: Unity and Diversity"; ibid.
141 Weiss, 29.
142 Maqsood, 45–46.

2. To Pray (*Salat*)

Symbolizing the five steps of Muhammad on the night of his ascent into the seven heavens, Muslim prayers are performed five times a day—at dawn, at noon, in the midafternoon, at dusk, and two hours after sunset.[143] Men and women are to be clean and modestly dressed during prayer. Women should not wear makeup or perfume. Often using a prayer mat, adherents face toward Mecca in a ritual called *qiblah*. They remove their shoes, then they stand, kneel, bow, lie prostrate, and repeat certain suras.

Once a week, on Fridays at noon, Muslim men are expected to attend services at the mosque. Sometimes believers carry prayer beads, similar to the Catholic rosary. The ninety-nine beads represent the ninety-nine revealed names of Allah. The worshiper repeats, "Glory be to Allah. Thanks be to Allah. God is most great" thirty-three times each, as he or she passes over the beads.[144]

3. To Give Alms (*Zakat*)

One-fortieth (2.5 percent) of a Muslim's annual income is considered an "alms tax" that must be given to the poor.

4. To Fast During Ramadan (*Sawm*)

The highest of holy seasons in Islam is the Muslim's ninth month. In honor of Muhammad's receiving the Koran during this month, fasting is required every day during sunlight hours. Muslims must abstain from eating, drinking, smoking, and sexual intercourse.[145]

5. To Make the Pilgrimage to Mecca (*Haj*)

Muslims are expected to visit Mecca at least once in their lifetimes and pay homage to Allah at the temple. Millions of Muslims make this trip each year. There are two types of pilgrimages. The smaller trip does not correspond with specific dates. It is called '*umra*.

---

143 Dean C. Halverson, *The Compact Guide to World Religions* (Minneapolis, MN: Bethany House Publishers, 1996), 107.
144 Maqsood, 58.
145 Halverson, 107.

The second kind of pilgrimage is made during Dhu l-hijjah, the last month of the Islamic moon calendar. *Haj* is the honorary title for those who go to Mecca during the great pilgrimage each year. Pilgrims do not shave, comb their hair, use perfume, or cut their nails or hair. They may not hunt, argue, or have sexual intercourse.[146] Dressed in standardized white garments and sandals meant to diminish class distinction, pilgrims attempt to see or—if they are fortunate enough—touch and kiss the Black Stone, a bowling ball–sized object, possibly of meteoric origin, that has been set in a silver collar in a corner of the Kabah.[147]

The Kabah in Mecca has been the central shrine of Islam since CE 624. Approximately fifty feet high, it is situated in the middle of the

The Grand Mosque of Mecca (in the 19th century)

1. The well of Zamzam
2. The place of Abraham
3. The Matâf, the open area to walk around the Ka'bah
4. The Ka'bah
5. Entrance to the Ka'bah and the Black Stone
6. Stairs to the water taps of the Zamzam well

7. Path on which pilgrims run seven times (*sa'y*) between Safâ and Marwah. Today a pedestrian tunnel within the Mosque encloses the path, and the hills Safâ and Marwah are also both integrated into the grounds.

---

146 Weiss, 37.
147 John Renard, *Seven Doors To Islam: Spirituality and the Religious Life of Muslims* (Berkeley, CA: University of California Press, 1996), 39.

Grand Mosque as an empty, windowless room with marble walls. At the east corner of the Kabah, the Black Stone is embedded into the wall about five feet above the ground. Its surface has been polished smooth by centuries of contact with hands and lips. The outer walls of the *bayt Allah* ("House of God") are hung with a black brocade blanket (*kiswah*). Embroidered on the brocade in gold thread are numerous Koranic verses. Each year, the expensive covering is replaced with a new one in a festival ritual.[148]

What Is the Holy Jihad?

Considered by some to be the "sixth pillar" of the faith, *jihad* has become the center of many modern debates. In recent years, the practice has come under international scrutiny, because so many terrorist attacks have been linked with the concept of jihad.

Author Anne Cooper explains the concept of jihad as meaning "to struggle to the utmost of one's capacity." Various interpretations exist:

- A holy war and defense of Islam
- The raiding and conquest that took place during the early spread of Islam
- A modern call to propagate Islam
- Personal self-discipline[149]

The word *jihad* literally means "efforts on God's path," but it is roughly translated as "holy war." In practice, the idea is applied to what has become known as the *greater* jihad or the *lesser* jihad. The greater jihad is an inner struggle used to bring a person closer to Allah. In one sense, it is similar to the Christian "wrestling" of Ephesians 6:10–12. The lesser jihad involves militant jihad against the infidels (e.g., Jews and Christians) who resist the expansion of Islam or who pose a threat against it. Of course, it is to the ideology of lesser jihad that the fundamentalists of Islam rally today.

---

148 Weiss, 36.
149 Cooper, 127.

Here is the dilemma for Christians who talk to Muslims about the issue of jihad. The Muslim and the Christian are often talking about different applications or interpretations of the word *jihad*. The Muslim may be talking about the value of the greater jihad (inner struggle), whereas the Christian is often thinking about the atrocity of those who carry out the lesser jihad (acts of terror).

For many Muslims, a *jihad* is supposed to be primarily an inner struggle, rather than a military one. These are Muslims who consider the modern application of jihad to be the struggle within one's own heart, the attempt to bring oneself in accord with the will of God. The various means used to conduct this struggle are prayer, study of the Koran, and various other forms of inner-worldly asceticism.[150] For these adherents, who aspire to the highest ideals of the inner struggle to draw themselves closer to God, the modern radicals who are justifying terror attacks in the name of jihad are actually hijacking the religion.

However, in the early history of Islam, the application of jihad could be *both* the greater and the lesser idea. Often in the early years, with the expansion of Islam, it was interpreted to mean military action, sometimes including what today would be considered terrorism.

This military action could be either offensive or defensive warfare. An offensive jihad was supposed to be led by a legitimate successor of the prophet Muhammad. That becomes a problem today, because some think that no legitimate successor exists in our modern era. Therefore that tenet must indicate that jihad should only be defensive in nature.[151]

However, Islamic fundamentalists twist this idealism by reasoning that the best defense is a good offense. They say they have taken up arms to defend Islam against the encroaching influence of the West. Therefore, no place outside of Islam is safe.

After the attacks on September 11, 2001, in America, various Muslim leaders appeared on television to temper the view that ji-

---

150 John Kelsay, *Islam and War: A Study in Comparative Ethics* (Louisville, KY: Westminister / John Knox Press, 1993, 34.
151 Weiss, 39.

had was "bad." They denied that a militant jihad was part of true Islamic teaching. Most of these were American Muslims who did not speak for the majority of Muslims outside the United States. Most American Muslims do not have a violent, militant, offensive, or even fundamental view of jihad. They appreciate the freedoms they have in the United States. Plus, they don't want neighboring Americans to think that Islam could have such offensive doctrines like that of a justified holy war. But it actually does.

Muslims cannot deny the overt militant application of the jihad. Muhammad himself led the first military jihad. Afterward, a series of jihads broadened Islamic influence across the Middle East, including in Jerusalem, which had been under Christian control. These Muslim conquests continued west into Africa, east into Asia, and they penetrated Europe three times.

In his book *In the Shadow of the Prophet: Struggle for the Soul of Islam,* Milton Viorst writes: "Muslims, from Islam's earliest days, were bound by the Prophet's precedent to wage jihad, 'holy war' to promote the faith. The very name given to the non-Islamic world—Dar al-Harb, the 'domain of war'—reaffirmed this duty. But over the centuries the religious scholars have softened the duty, thereby enabling Islam to coexist with its diverse neighbors."[152]

Author Bernard Lewis was interviewed in the *Wall Street Journal* shortly after the September 11 attacks. He noted that jihad typically goes beyond a spiritual and moral struggle. "The more common interpretation, and that of the overwhelming majority of the classical jurist and commentators, presents jihad as an armed struggle for Islam against infidels and apostates. Unlike 'crusade' it has maintained its religious and military connotation into modern times."[153] This was the reason behind Osama bin Laden's 1998 declaration of war against the United States. Today, it is quite obvious that the concept of jihad has a very militant interpretation by fundamentalist Muslims. This is the driving concept that is currently used to radicalize and create Islamic terrorists.

---

152 Viorst, 16.
153 Bernard Lewis, "Jihad vs. Crusade," *Wall Street Journal* (September 27, 2001).

Mark Gabriel, author and Islamic historian, estimates that 60 percent of the Koran is related to the topic of jihad, and that modern Islamic radicals—fundamentalists—desire to practice Islam and jihad the way that Muhammad did. He says that despite the differences between modern radical groups, there are certain principles, or philosophies, that fuel these groups and that draw in new generations of radical Muslims. Here is his list:

The Five Pillars of Radical Islamic Philosophy[154]

1. Obey no law but Islamic law.
2. Infidels are all around.
3. Islam must rule.
4. Jihad is the only way to win.
5. Faith is the reason.

It is important to remember that there are peaceful Muslims in the world and that there are very rational, intelligent Muslims who want to bring Islam out of the dark ages. One of the most-respected Muslims in America today is Dr. Zhudi Jasser, who founded the American Islamic Forum for Democracy after the attacks on 9/11. He is an outspoken critic of radical and political Islam. His constant call of reform of Islam illustrates to the world that there are wise, dedicated Muslims who do not like what has been happening to their religion. After the mass shooting in the Orlando nightclub on June 12, 2016, by Omar Mateen, a shooter who killed forty-nine people and injured fifty-three others, and then made a pledge to ISIS on a 911 call, Jasser was interviewed on Fox News. Here are a few of the statements that were reported concerning what he said:

> Dr. Zuhdi Jasser said that if the Orlando mass shooting was, indeed, linked to radical Islam, then it should be a wakeup call for moderate Muslims. . . . "At which point are we Muslims going to look in the mirror and declare war on what has declared war on us as Americans?" Jasser said. "That's really what needs to happen." . . . Jasser said the enemy isn't violent extremism or "lone wolves," but a global ideology of "political Islam." . . . "It

---

154 Mark A. Gabriel, 11, 18.

attacks free speech, it attacks free secular countries," Jasser said, asserting that this particular gay nightclub was targeted because homophobia is central to "political Islam." . . . He said it was time for Muslims to stop denying the problem and confront this "Islamo-nationalism." . . . "Muslims need to be part of it. We can't get past it without real reforms to get our Sharia Islamic law out of the thirteenth century in which it's stuck."[155]

The Six Major Doctrines of Islam

1. God

There is one true God, Allah, who is all seeing, all knowing, and all-powerful. If someone associates a partner with God, it is an unforgivable sin called *shirk*. Sura 4:51 says, "Verily, God will not forgive the union of other gods with Himself."[156] Thus, the Christian teaching of the Trinity is highly offensive to Muslims because they misunderstand how Christians view the Oneness of God.

2. Angels

The chief angel is Gabriel, who is said to have appeared to Muhammad. There is also a fallen angel named Shaitan (from the Hebrew, Satan). His followers are the *jinn* (demons).[157] These jinn are where the concept of the "genie" comes from. It is also believed that each person has two angels assigned to their life: one recording the good deeds, and one the bad.

3. Holy Books

Five holy books are mentioned in the Koran:

- The scrolls of Abraham, which are now lost
- The *Tawrat* (the Torah), given to the prophet Moses
- The *Zabur* (the Psalms), given to the prophet David

---

155 Fox News blog, "Jasser: Muslims Must Declare War on Radical Islam," *Fox News Insider* (June 12, 2016); insider.foxnews.com.
156 *The Koran*, 54.
157 Fritz Ridenour, *So What's the Difference?* (Ventura, CA: Regal Books, 2001), 79.

- The *Injil* (the Gospels), given to the prophet Jesus
- The Koran, which was revealed to the prophet Muhammad

The Hadith is also sacred to Muslims, but it is not mentioned in the Koran. It was written later. This book is comprised of the words or acts of Muhammad from secondary sources. These are considered "traditions" by Muslims. The word *Hadith* refers not only to the collection of traditions, but to the individual traditions themselves. These *hadith* inform of the *sunna* (customary practice) of Muhammad and of those who were his companions.[158]

Muslims believe that the Bible is badly corrupted. Therefore the Koran supersedes all previous revelations and is Allah's final revelation to man.

4. The Prophets

Muhammad is the greatest of the twenty-six prophets mentioned in the Koran.[159] Tradition suggests that there have been 124,000 prophets who have visited various cultures throughout history, bringing the true teachings of monotheism and Allah. This is a symbolic number meaning there has been an infinite number of prophets.[160]

5. The End Times

On the Day of Judgment, Allah will reward or punish people according to their deeds. The results will be either heaven or hell. The concept of heaven is referred to only a bit in Islam. Sura 55 indi-

---

158 John Bowker, ed., *The Oxford Dictionary of World Religions* (Oxford, England: Oxford University Press, 1997), 398.

159 Ridenour says that the Koran lists twenty-eight prophets, 80. Yet, Maqsood, who is a Muslim, indicates that there are twenty-six prophets mentioned in the Koran. These include biblical prophets such as Noah, Abraham, Moses, John the Baptist, and Jesus. But there are three—Hud, Salih, and Shu'aib—who are not from the biblical source. Their lives and origins are apparently unknown. Maqsood, 37.

160 Armstrong, 8.

cates that it will be quite a place—for men, that is—full of beautiful women, pillowed couches, flowing fountains, and plenty of fruit to eat in luscious gardens of pleasure.

The Koran greatly emphasizes the subject of hell. It is mentioned in almost every sura.

6. Predestination

Orthodox (Sunni) Islam holds to a fatalistic, pessimistic world-view. Devout Muslims constantly make decisions with the comment, "If Allah wills it," because orthodox Islam teaches the absolute pre-destination of both good and evil. All thoughts, words, and deeds, whether good or evil, were foreseen, foreordained, determined, and decreed from all eternity. Everything that happens takes place according to what has been written about it.[161]

Orthodox Islam also denies people the ability to freely choose or reject Allah. This extreme view of predestination causes a great deal of theological controversy, even among Muslims, because it creates natural contradictions within the Koran and eliminates human responsibility. At that point, God becomes the Author of both good *and* evil, which some have used to justify pantheism. Shiites do not believe in predestination, but in free-will choice as explained below.

The Sects of Islam

There have been many schisms within Islam. At the time of the prophet's life, differences were solved through military muscle and Muhammad's revelations. The prophet's army won the battles, and his revelations became the law. After Muhammad's death, the caliphs created divisions in the religion. Today, the Sunnis and Shiites have become the two major sects of modern Islam. Eventually, the Sufi also emerged. A simplified and general way of considering these three sects is this:

---

161 Annemarie Schimmel and Abdoljavad Falaturi, *We Believe in One God* (New York, NY: Seabury Press, 1979), 85.

- Sunni are orthodox, led by majority consensus.
- Shiites are radical, led by specific authority.
- Sufi are mystical, led by individuals' quests.

The Sunnites (Sunni)

This moderate, orthodox sect of Islam comprises approximately 80 to 85 percent of Muslim believers.[162] They focus on the traditions of Islam. The word *sunnah* means "customs."

Author Ruqaiyyah Maqsood says, "The life and example of the Prophet are known as the Sunnah."[163] Also included are the teachings of the Koran and Hadith, and also the teachings of subsequent religious scholars throughout history. The consensus of these scholars is often considered to be the will of God. The Sunni have a tendency to separate religion from politics. The Sunni elect the best leader. He does not have to be a descendant of Muhammad. The word *imam* to them simply refers to anyone leading or teaching in a mosque.

The Shiites (Shias)

This radical arm of Islam comprises about 15 to 20 percent of Islam. Originally, they disagreed with the Sunnis on who should rule the followers of Islam after Muhammad died. The Sunni accepted the four caliphs who succeeded Muhammad. They were considered the best men in the community to lead, regardless of their actual kinship with Muhammad. On the other side, the Shiites believed that only a member of Muhammad's direct blood-related family should succeed him. Since Muhammad had no son, it was thought that the

---

162 Halverson says the number is 80 percent, 105. Yet Cooper estimates that 90 percent of Islam is Sunni, 179. The statistics used obviously come from different sources, possibly employing varying standards of measurement. All of the sources that I researched used the number of 10 percent for the Shiites. Add to this the Sufi and many other little sects within Islam, and I think that using 80 percent for the Sunni is probably nearer the mark. Wikipedia says that there are between 10 and 13 percent Shiites worldwide; https://en.wikipedia.org/wiki/Islamic_schools_and_branches#Shia_Islam (accessed March 31, 2016).
163 Maqsood, 109.

only rightful successor would be Ali, the prophet's cousin and the husband of Fatima, a daughter of Muhammad. These specially appointed family leaders were called *imams*. According to the Shiites, these political and spiritual rulers of Islam were infallible vessels of God's light. Today, Shiites add to the creed of Islam the words "and Ali is the friend of God."[164] So, their *Shahadah* would be: *There is no god but Allah and Muhammad is his messenger and Ali is the friend of God.*

After Ali was assassinated in CE 661, the party of 'Ali (the Arabic word *shi'at* comes from 'Ali) was formed. The Shiites disavowed the Umayyad family and recognized Ali's son, Hasan, as the leader. But Hasan had no ambition, so they eventually acknowledged his younger brother, Husayn ibn Ali, as the imam. On October 10 in the year CE 680, soldiers of the Umayyad caliph massacred Husayn ibn Ali and a small group in the Iraqi desert of Kerbala. Husayn had been deserted by many of the Shiites. Today, the Shiites mourn for that sin on October 10 every year in what they call Ashura, a ritual in which devotees beat themselves.

After Husayn, other imams were recognized, but eventually this conflict caused another schism. Today, there are different Shiite groups with slightly varying views.

- Fiver Shiites (Zaydites)—moderates who elect descendants of 'Ali to lead them
- Sevener Shiites (Ishmailites)—esoteric and full of strife
- Twelver Shiites (Imamites)—the largest group, these people have "a strong desire for salvation," thinking that the twelfth imam is the savior who will come out of hiding at the end of time[165]

The Shiite salvation concept bucks against the Sunni belief of predestination. Shiites believe in free choice. In addition, upon the return of the twelfth imam, Mahdi, a divine kingdom of justice will be established. Consequently, Shiites question the legitimacy of earthly political powers.

---

164 Cooper, 181.
165 Weiss, 68.

Sunnis regard Shiites with disdain. They see them as intolerant, speculative, and extremists who preach revolution, martyrdom, and terrorism. Shiites embrace the militant interpretation of jihad and are the ones who call the West "the Great Satan."[166] It is interesting that the Sunnis see the Shiites as extremists, however, because it was actually nineteen Sunni terrorists belonging to al-Qaeda who hijacked the planes on September 11, 2001, and attacked America

The Ayatollah Khomeini of Iran was a Shiite leader who spoke out against the West. Shiites currently hold the largest percentages of the population in Iran, Azerbaijan, Iraq, and Bahrain, but they also have significant populations in Yemen, Lebanon, Afghanistan, Kuwait, and Pakistan.[167]

The Sufi

Sufism has gnostic and pantheistic tendencies. Sufis are not concerned about traditional Islam or even monotheism, but they often practice animism and spiritism.

Many conservative Muslims reject this mystical sect of Islam. In their book, *Tales from the Land of the Sufis*, Mojdeh Bayet and Mohammad Ali Jamnia teach that Sufism has two major concepts: the unity of being—a concept that the universe is a manifestation of God's attributes and, as such, is not separate from Him—and the order of Sufi masters, who provide guidance for people who are seeking God.[168]

While orthodox Islam is concerned about ultimate truth, the nature of reality, and the way to heaven, Sufism is more concerned about day-to-day living and whatever works in the pursuit of God. An example could be: "A father with a sick son will ask the mullah to pray to God for him, tie an amulet to his arm to drive off evil spirits, and give him modern medicine to kill the germs—all at the same time."[169]

---

166 Maqsood, 24–25.
167 Weiss, ibid.
168 Bayat and Jamnia, 11.
169 J. Dudley Woodberry, ed., *Muslims and Christians on the Emmaus Road* (Monrovia, CA: MARC Publications, 1989), 49.

The Ancient Struggle

What is often overlooked today as various wars erupt between the East and the West, or Muslim-dominated and other nations, is the ancient conflict between the Sunni and the Shia that boils beneath the surface of most conflicts involving nations with significant Islamic populations. Paul Vallely, a reporter for the *Independent*, expresses the real tension behind many of the conflicts in the Middle East:

> What most of the crucibles of conflict in the Middle East have in common is that Sunni Muslims are on one side of the disagreement and Shia Muslims on the other. Oman is unusual because its Sunni and Shia residents are outnumbered by a third sect, the Ibadis, who constitute more than half the population. In many countries, the Sunni and the Shia are today head-to-head.
>
> The rift between the two great Islamic denominations runs like a tectonic fault-line along what is known as the Shia Crescent, starting in Lebanon in the north and curving through Syria and Iraq to the Gulf and to Iran and further east.
>
> The division between Sunni and Shia Muslims is the oldest in the Middle East—and yet it is one which seems increasingly to be shaping the destiny of this troubled region as thousands of devotees from both sides pour into Syria. Jihadist al-Qa'ida volunteers on the Sunni side and Hezbollah militants on the Shia, are joining what is fast becoming a transnational civil war between the two factions.[170]

In 2011, what came to be known as the Arab Spring took the world by surprise as it seemed that many rigid Islamic regimes were seeking more of a free, democratic method of government, as Tunisia, Egypt, Libya, Syria, Yemen, and Bahrein erupted daily in the news media sources. Yet, what began as a season of hope ended in anguish and worldwide drama as ISIS rose up as a fundamentalist Sunni response. It was built on the foundation of Al Qaeda, but it went much further in declaring itself the new caliphate and calling for faithful Sunni Muslims everywhere to pledge allegiance, not to countries with geopolitical boundaries, but to the ideology of the

---

170 Paul Vallely, "The vicious schism between Sunni and Shia has been poisoning Islam for 1,400 years—and it is getting worse," *Independent* (February 19, 2014); www.independent.co.uk/.

Islamic State.

The Sharia

The Sharia is the general title for Islamic law—the foundation from Allah for all of creation. More than a legal system, the Sharia is based on obligations found in the Koran that guide people to walk in Allah's will. The Sharia addresses fifty major areas of one's life, including religious practices, family law, inheritance, trade, customs, traditions, and civil and criminal law. It even includes such topics as greetings, dress, and what to say when someone sneezes. Whereas Christians *model* their lives after Jesus, Muslims *require* this conduct. Faithfulness to the law determines one's eternal destiny in heaven or in hell.[171]

For the first three hundred years after Muhammad's death, Islamic jurists argued about the many religious and legal aspects of the Koran and the Hadith. When Muhammad died, the so-called law was only a hodgepodge of rules and admonitions. Thinking that they needed a more comprehensive system, the jurists divided and created four major Sunni schools of Sharia law:

- The liberal school of the Hanafites
- The moderate school of the Shafiites
- The uncompromising, dogmatic school of the Hanbalites
- The school of the Malikites, based primarily on seventh-century community practices in Medina
- The minor school of the Ẓāhirī, followed by several minority communities and other smaller schools of thought

The Shiites have their own schools of jurisprudence, the largest being the Jafarite school of law. This is the jurisprudence that the Twelver Shiites embrace, and it teaches that religious leaders can interpret divine law (God's will) anew. The Sunnis disagree

---

171 Viorst, 142. He contends that both Jewish and Christian law lost much of its social role because they were in cultures dominated by secular governments, such as Rome. Islamic law orients the faith to the past and points Muslim society into an idyllic seventh-century time of the Prophet. Muslim utopia is historic rather than spiritual in nature.

and believe that no new interpretation has been available since the tenth century.

The leading Shiite imams can earn the title *ayatollah*, or "shadow of God." Thus, the Ayatollah Khomeini acted in accordance with Allah's law when he overthrew the pro-Western Shah Muhammad Reza Pahlevi in 1979. Before the revolution, Khomeini wrote the following while he was in exile:

> The entire system of government and administration, together with the necessary laws, lies ready for you. If the administration of the country calls for taxes, Islam has established them provision; and if laws are needed, Islam has established them all. There is no need for you after establishing a government, to sit down and draw up laws, or, like rulers who worship foreigners and are infatuated with the West, run after others to borrow their laws. Everything is ready and waiting. All that remains is to draw up ministerial programs, and that can be accomplished with the help and cooperation of consultants and advisers who are experts in different fields, gathered together in a consultative assembly.[172]

Was Khomeini's experiment of the Islamic state successful? No. When he returned and overthrew the Shah, a half million Iranian professionals fled the country; ten thousand people—including women and children—were executed; and rebellion, intervention, and war cost Iran a half million lives and two million refugees.[173] Is it any wonder that the Iranians elected the moderate cleric Mohammed Khatami in May 1997 by a clear 70 percent? The concept of the Islamic state under Sharia law had failed.[174]

Unfortunately, many other nations are struggling to bring the Sharia into a place of absolute law. Persecution and intolerance is currently manifesting among many of those citizens. At the beginning of the century in Indonesia, the rise of fundamentalist and militant groups forced women to wear headscarves. They also raided

---

172 Imam Khomeini, *Islamic Government*, "Program for the Establishment of an Islamic Government," in Iman Khomeini (Hamid Algar, trans.), *Islam and Revolution: Writings and Declarations* (London: KRI, 1981), 137–138.
173 Lewis, 392.
174 Viorst, 174, 202.

hotel rooms to validate proof of marriage. Alcohol and discotheques were forbidden.[175]

Milton Viorst wrote, "Fundamentalism has remained on the agenda, not only among the Arabs but among Muslims everywhere. Clearly, most Muslims feel less threatened by their fundamentalism than most Christians and Jews feel by theirs. If fundamentalism is to win out among any of the 'Abrahamic' faiths—Judaism, Christianity, and Islam are all said to descend from the patriarch Abraham—it will surely have its first triumph in Islam."[176]

In early 2016, a Saudi court sentenced a poet, Ashraf Fayadh, to eight years in prison and eight hundred lashes. He was lucky, because his sentence was reduced from beheading. This was for the crime of the content he had written in his poems and an illicit relationship he had had with a woman. In 2014, a blogger named Raef Badawi received ten years in prison, a large fine, and one thousand blows for criticizing the religious establishment. These are but two examples of modern extremism in Sharia law. Freedom of speech—the ability to speak out against this religion and its archaic, abusive laws—is being tested on many fronts today, including in democratic societies that are giving in to the influence and pressure of Islam.

175 Devi Asmarani, "Shariah law? Jakarta offers new criminal code instead," *Straight Times Indonesian Bureau* (October 19, 2001); library.ohiou.ed/in-pubs/2001/10/19/0065.html.
176 Viorst, 20.

CHAPTER 7

The Koran

I studied the Quran a great deal. I came away from that study with the conviction that, by and large, there have been few religions in the world as deadly to men as that of Muhammad.[177]

—Alexis de Tocqueville

The Writing of the Koran

The word *Koran* means "to recite." It can be spelled various ways: *Qur'an*, *Qor'an*, etc., but for the purpose of consistency, this book uses the word *Koran*.

One of Muhammad's maxims was "Give not way to the infidels, but by means of this Koran strive against them with a mighty strife" (Sura 25:54). Muhammad used both the pen and the sword to bring influence, but it certainly was his pen that changed the world.

According to Islamic tradition, the Koran was revealed to Muhammad by the angel Gabriel between the years CE 610–632. Scribes wrote the revelations down on everything from pieces of papyrus to stones, palm leaves, shoulder bones, animal ribs, leather, and boards.[178] All of these were collected after his death, and soon, numerous versions were circulating among the population. Caliph

---

177 Alexis de Tocqueville, Olivier Zunz, Alan S. Kahan, *The Toqueville Reader*, Blackwell Publishing (2002), 229.
178 *The Concise Encyclopedia of Islam*, Cyril Classe, ed. (London: Stacey International, 1989), 230.

Uthman caused great controversy by authorizing one version and having many of the rest destroyed. This version became the official Koran. The other versions that survived show variants of individual suras and verses. This has caused a scholarly debate within modern Islam, but it has also closed the ancient manuscripts to Western scholastic criticism.[179]

Sura 13:37 says that the Koran is "a code in the Arabic tongue." Hence, Arabic was the perfect language of the Koran, and any "translation" would simply be an interpretation.[180] Interestingly, author Arthur Jeffrey in his book, *The Foreign Vocabulary of the Quran*, cites more than one hundred foreign non-Arabic words in the Koran.[181] The suras (chapters) are not in chronological order and are without organization. The first one was probably Sura 96:

> Read! In the name of your Lord who created:
> He created man from a clinging form.
> Read! Your Lord is the Most Bountiful One
> Who taught by the pen,
> Who taught man what he did not know. (Sura 96:1–5, Haleem)

Muhammad was familiar with the Bible stories, even though he called himself the "unlettered Prophet" in Sura 7:156 and adamantly denied that he received any information from outside sources. J. M. Rodwell, in his commentarial notes on the Koran, wrote: "There can, however, be no doubt that Muhammad—in spite of assertions to the contrary, with the view of proving his inspiration—was well-acquainted with the Bible stories."[182] Rodwell considers Muhammad to be sincere in his quest, but ultimately "self-deceived."[183]

The Koran consists of 114 suras. The number of verses is debatable. Islamic scholars have assigned 6616, 6217, or even 6666

---

179 Morey cites examples of Koranic versions, textual problems, and cover-up stories, chapter 9.
180 *The Oxford Dictionary of World Religions*, John Bowker, ed. (Oxford: Oxford University Press, 1997), 786.
181 Arthur Jeffrey, *The Foreign Vocabulary of the Quran* (Baroda: Oriental Institute, 1938), no. 79.
182 J. M. Rodwell, *The Koran*, notes, 448.
183 Ibid., 500.

or other numbers to the suras, depending on how they divide the phrases into verses. The verses are known as *ayas* (meaning "signs"). Each is thought to be a sign from God.[184] The most popular tradition divides the suras into four periods:

- Early Meccan
- Middle Meccan
- Late Meccan
- Medinan[185]

After the first sura, there was an intermission of six months to three years. During this time, Muhammad struggled with whether or not the revelations and voices were from God. His seizures were a constant challenge for both him and for those who knew him. He debated with people who thought he was demon-possessed. Suras 7:181 and 81:20–29 show that people, even some of his companions, thought that his doctrine was from Satan. In sura 69:40–47, Muhammad makes the demand that he be considered an apostle and not a poet. The *jinn* were believed to inspire the poets.[186] Still, the strong possibility of demonic influence was demonstrated by his:

1. Concern over his seizures
2. Manipulation of his revelations for his own gain
3. Dishonesty in the Koranic sources
4. Brutality toward those who did not embrace his message
5. Provocation of a spirit of warfare against Christians and Jews

The Arabs of the day obviously had a problem with his assertion of the Koran's divine inspiration. For example, in Sura 3:181, Muhammad defends himself against claims that he was a liar by proclaiming that he was an apostle. In Sura 67:9, he imagined himself in heaven on Judgment Day, hearing the voices of those who did not believe him. The unbelievers would then be forced to confess that they thought he was a liar and full of delusion. Below I list a

---

184 Cooper, 78.
185 Alan Jones, Introduction to *The Koran* (Rutland, VT: Charles E. Tuttle Co., Inc., 1995), xx.
186 Alan Jones, Introduction to *The Koran*, xiii.

few verses that, by extrapolation, reveal obvious Arab resistance and rebuttals of his message:

> But when our clear signs are recited to them, they who look not forward to meet Us, say, "Bring a different Koran from this, or make some change in it." (Sura 10:16)
>
> This is no new fiction, but a confirmation of previous scriptures, and an explanation of all things, and guidance and mercy to those who believe. (Sura 12:111)
>
> The disbelievers say, "This [Koran] can only be a lie he has forged with the help of others"—they themselves have done great wrong and told lies, "It is just ancient fables, which he has had written down: they are dictated to him morning and evening." (Sura 25:4-5, Haleem)

It is evident that many people at first did not like what Muhammad was saying. They also apparently accused him of writing fiction, making up fraudulent stories, and borrowing writings from ancient sources. This is not easy criticism to take, when one is trying to convince people of a divine revelation from heaven. So, he challenged them:

> Will they say, "He hath forged it [the Koran] himself?" Nay, rather it is that they believed not. Let them produce a discourse like it, if they speak the Truth. (Sura 52:32–33)
>
> Then bring a Sura like it; and call on whom ye can beside God, if ye speak truth. (Sura 10:39)

Some took Muhammad up on his challenge. Nadir ibn Haritha arranged some stories of Persian kings into suras and recited them.[187] Hamzah ben-Ahed wrote a book against the Koran. Another man, Maslema, wrote a book that caused a "defection of great number of Mussulmans."[188]

---

187 Canon Sell, *Studies in Islam* (London: Diocesan Press, 1928), 208.
188 John McClintock and James Strong, *Cyclopedia of Biblical, Theological, and Ecclesiastical Literature* (Baker Book House, 1981), V: 152.

Remember, Muhammad did have a commitment to driving out any worship other than that of his tribe's god, Allah. He also wanted to bring unity to the scattered Arab tribes and become their leader. Yet, that does not necessarily mean that he had God's approval, character, or inspiration.

The Perfect Tablet

The Koran displays a passion on behalf of Muhammad for Allah, such as in mercy and compassion. Muhammad appreciates the plight of the poor and tries to alleviate their burdens. There are admonitions toward high moral standards. He also improved the rights of women by forbidding female infanticide, a practice used widely in that region prior to his writings. However, Muhammad did not see women as equal to men. He confirmed the inferiority of women in Arabian society in sura 4:37–38, pronouncing that men have the right to "scourge" any wives who are disobedient. The Koran also endorses polygamy of up to four wives.

Some suras appear to promote peace and goodwill between Arabs and their non-Muslim neighbors. Those must have been revealed during the early years, when Muhammad hoped to influence the Jews, Christians, and rebellious Arabs by his entreaties. However, by the end, he had become a full-fledged warrior-prophet.

The Koran is supposedly the *umm al-kittab*, the preexistent scripture preserved in heaven. It was supposedly uncreated. Muhammad said: "Yet it is a glorious Koran, written on the preserved Tablet" (Sura 85:21–22). But the Mu'tazilites of the ninth century, a body of dissident theologians, challenged this thinking by teaching that only Allah was uncreated, because he has existed forever; therefore, the Koran must be created.[189] Yet, Muslim consensus has not embraced this view and still holds that the Koran is "eternal, uncreated, and perfect."[190]

Numerous narratives in the Koran reveal the evolution of Muhammad's two primary doctrines:

189 Viorst notes that after a tumultuous battle, Orthodox Islam won against Mu'tazilism. The teachings of the dissident theologians offered a free-will view of life, but Orthodox Islam denied this and only offered fatalism, 87–88.
190 *The Oxford Dictionary of World Religions*, 786.

1. God sent many prophets over the ages to many people groups with the same monotheistic message.
2. Muhammad is the last and greatest messenger, specifically sent to the Arabs.

Of this "perfect tablet," many non-Muslims have had a problem with its readability. For those who would attempt to read it, it's helpful to read out loud.

Scholar and historian Thomas Carlyle once said of it:

> It is as toilsome reading as I ever undertook, a wearisome, confused jumble, crude, incondite.[191]

Salomon Reinach, a French archaeologist, wrote about the Koran:

> From the literary point of view, the Koran has little merit. Declamation, repetition, puerility, a lack of logic and coherence strike the unprepared reader at every turn. It is humiliating to the human intellect to think that this mediocre literature has been the subject of innumerable commentaries, and that millions of men are still wasting time absorbing it.[192]

Even a Muslim scholar, Ali Dashi, remarked:

> The Qor'an was badly edited and its contents are very obtusely arranged. All students of the Qor'an wonder why the editors did not use the natural and logical method of ordering by date of revelation.[193]

The Koran constantly changes topics. Also, many suras appear to be dialogue between people who challenged Muhammad's revelations and what appear to be his own meditative, polemic responses.

Since the time of Muhammad, many others have devised fables and claimed them to not only supersede the Koran, but also super-

191 Quoted by Professor H. A. Gibb in *Mohammedanism: An Historical Survey*, 37.
192 Salomon Reinach, *Orpheus: A History of Religions* (1909).
193 Ali Dashti, *23 Years: A Study of the Prophetic Career of Mohammad* (London: George Allen & Unwin, 1985), 28.

sede the Old and New Testaments. Among them is Baha'u'llah, the founder of the Baha'ism, who wrote *The Kitab-I-iqan*. He claimed to be the twelfth imam, the hidden Mahdi returned, the fulfillment of an unfulfilled prophecy of the Shiite community.

Many modern cult, New Age, and occult adherents could be included in the list of those who say that their revelation supersedes not only the Bible, but the Koran as well. The point is that just because Muhammad received a revelation, it proves nothing about God's authorship of the Koran. His continuous argumentative rebuttals about the Koran being from God are more of an indictment for the opposite.

Problems with the Koran

The Koran is represented as a book that should not be doubted (Sura 2:2). It is without contradictions, according to the prophet: "Can they not consider the Koran? Were it from any other than God, they would surely have found in it many contradictions" (Sura 4:83).

There are plenty of internal problems, illogical statements, errors, and contradictions within the Koran. For instance, there are the strange verses about Allah changing people into scouted apes and swine (Sura 2:62; 5:64; 7:164). These are primarily about Jews who would not endorse Muhammad's leadership. There is a debate among scholars as to whether this was to be taken figuratively or literally, in the sense that Allah would actually turn them into apes and swine, but be that as it may, it is not uncommon for Muslim parents today to teach their children that Jews are apes and swine.[194] Another example is that the Koran says that Solomon talked with birds and ants before a host of *jinn* and men (Sura 27:15–19).

With the Bible

There are many discrepancies between the Koran and the Bible. This is significant because the Koran is supposedly built on the former, valid, God-given revelations to the Jews and Christians. In the

---

194 James M. Arlandson, "Did Allah transform Jews into apes and pigs?"; answering-islam.org (accessed on April 4, 2016).

Koran, Muhammad admonishes Muslims to respect the Book and the "people of the book"—referring to Jews and Christians. But then he changes his stance: "Fight against those who have been given the Scripture as believeth not in Allah" (Sura 9:29).

The Koran alters numerous Old Testament accounts. First, for example, in Sura 2:93, we find that two angels named "Harut" and "Marut" were present at the tower of Babel. However, the biblical account, found in Genesis 11, does not mention these angels, even though it was written two thousand years before the Koran. Where did this information come from?

Second, numerous suras state that the angels in the Garden of Eden were ordered by Allah to prostrate themselves and worship Adam, but Eblis (Satan) refused to do so because of his pride (Sura 7:10–21). If Allah is the only one deserving of worship, however, why would angels be asked to worship Adam? This is contradictory to the first of the Ten Commandments (Exodus 20:3–6).

Third, Muslims like to use the dubious account recorded in Sura 37:102–109 to argue that Ishmael was to be Abraham's sacrifice, rather than Isaac.

> When the boy was old enough to work with his father, Abraham said, "My son, I have seen myself sacrificing you in a dream. What do you think?" He said, "Do as you are commanded and, God willing, you will find me steadfast." When they had both submitted to God, and he had laid his son down on the side of his face, We called out to him, "Abraham, you have fulfilled the dream." This is how we reward those who do good—it was a test to prove [their true characters]—We ransomed his son with a momentous sacrifice, and We let him be praised by succeeding generations: "Peace be upon Abraham!" (Haleem).

Notice that no name is attached to the "son" in the passage, but Muslims proclaim him to be Ishmael rather than Isaac. However, Genesis 22 leaves no room for doubt: It was Isaac who was the promised son of Abraham and who was used to test the faithfulness of the patriarch.

With the Sources of the Revelations in the Koran

Alan Jones notes some of the problems with discussing the source information of the Koran in his introduction:

> Orthodox doctrine renders discussion of the sources of the Qur'an irrelevant for Muslims: the Qur'an is the word of God. They are also able to dismiss discrepancies between the Bible and the Qur'an by recourse of the doctrine that if there are differences between the Jewish, Christian, and Muslim versions of the Scripture the Jews and the Christians have mangled the Message and Muslims have not. This doctrinal stance is, however, not without problems. It is difficult to reconcile the very specific references to, for example, Muhammad's family (cf., for example, Q. 33:28–33) with the belief that each prophet has received the same message.
>
> For non-Muslims the Muslim standpoint is untenable, and non-Muslim scholars have given much thought to the question of how Muhammad might have acquired his knowledge of the Bible. The most commonly accepted view is that Muhammad received most of his information about biblical stories through informants who talked with him; that this material was digested, meditated on and then absorbed into what became the text. There are two passages in the Qur'an that support this view. [See Q 16:103 and Q 25:4.] . . . It should be added that there is some corroboration in *hadith* that Muhammad received stories and information from various individuals, including Jews and Christians.[195]

There are four significant contradictions that exist within the Koran itself about how Muhammad received the revelations that ultimately became the Koran:

1. Suras 53:2–18 and 81:19–24 say that Allah personally appeared to Muhammad.
2. The Holy Spirit brought the Koran, according to Suras 16:102 and 26:192–194.
3. Sura 15:7–8 implies that various angels brought down the revelations.
4. Sura 2:91–92 states that only one angel, Gabriel, brought the Koran. Some Muslims downplay this contradiction by call-

---

195 Alan Jones, Introduction to *The Koran*, xxv.

ing Gabriel the "Holy Spirit" (Sura 16:102), but this opens up the theological prospect of the Trinity, which the Koran flat-out denies.

With Associate Gods

Muhammad's alleged revelation that there is only one God [Allah] is somewhat shaky. Muhammad denies the doctrine of the Trinity in various Koranic passages (Suras 4:169 and 5:77). His misunderstanding of the doctrine was based on the concept of adding "associate gods." He was supposedly more interested in protecting the purity of the doctrine of the Oneness of God than in simply being in control and making people believe the way that he thought they should believe.

Yet, if this was actually true, then one might ask why Muhammad made the mistake of adding Allah's daughters—Al-Lat, Al-Ozza, and Al-Manat—to the worship list in a move to appease his tribe? As demonstrated in chapter 4, one of the earliest controversies was that Muhammad first prophesied that it was proper for his tribe to worship the daughters of Allah in Sura 53, but then he reversed course and changed the revelation in order to retain converts from other tribes. This nearly ended his career.

With the Trinity

In Matthew 28:18–19, the Lord Jesus said, "All authority has been given to Me in heaven and on earth. Go therefore and make disciples of all the nations, baptizing them in the name of the Father and of the Son and of the Holy Spirit." In Christian doctrine, these three represent the Trinity. The Trinity is the doctrine that within the nature of the one God there are three eternal Persons: God the Father, God the Son, and God the Holy Spirit. This doctrine shows unity within trinity. In Colossians 2:9, the apostle Paul wrote: "For in Him dwells all the fullness of the Godhead bodily." The *Him* referred to in this passage is Jesus Christ. Most Christians throughout history have embraced this doctrine, and it is central to the revelation of God. There are numerous passages in both the Old and New Testaments that affirm this doctrine.

While the word *trinity* is not found in the Bible, the usage of it comes from the second century and forward to help us understand the revelation of the nature of God. It is a theological construct that tries to explain the mysterious way that God has revealed Himself in the Bible.[196] A Muslim might say, "The word *trinity* is not in the Bible, and so it must not be true." One response might be to ask the Muslim if the word *electricity* is in either the Bible or the Koran. Of course it is not, but the truth of it is all around us.

Muslims are taught that Christians worship three gods because they do not understand the unity doctrine of the trinity. They do not believe that Jesus was God incarnate (in the flesh), and they say that God could not die on the cross because they do not understand the revelation of the Lamb of God taking away the sins of the world, nor the concept of a loving Savior who went to the cross for all men. When witnessing to a Muslim about these things, a Christian should not be surprised if these concepts are rejected. Even if a Muslim is open to hearing about these concepts, it will take time to walk them through the revelations of the Old and New Testaments that affirm the doctrines of the Trinity and of the deity of Jesus Christ. This is true of most people, Muslim or not.

However, from birth, Muslims have been taught the following sura. It is memorized. It is prayed. It is often used as a call to prayer. It is ingrained deep in their hearts. This passage not only stifles any openness to the doctrine of the Trinity but also to the concept of the deity of Christ.

> Say, "He is God the One, God the eternal. He begot no one nor was He begotten. No one is comparable to Him." (Sura 112:1–4, Haleem)

The We/Us Trinitarian Concepts

In consideration of the Koran and the topic of the Trinity, there are passages that potentially illustrate the plurality of God and stand in stark contrast to the above sura. Remember that Muslims believe

---

196 Abdul Saleeb, "Answering Misha 'al Al-Kadhi's question about Jesus," (January 20, 1985); answering-islam.org (accessed April 5, 2016).

that the Koran is perfect as God's direct revelation to Muhammad. They say that it is full of *signs*. Signs are important in understanding the revelation of God. In the following passages, notice the plural form used for Allah: *Us* and *We*.

> But when our clear signs are recited to them, they who look not forward to meet Us, say, "Bring a different Koran from this, or make some change in it." (Sura 10:16)
>
> It is a missive from the Lord of the worlds. But if Muhammad had fabricated concerning us any sayings, We had surely seized him by the right hand, and had cut through the vein of his neck. Nor would We have withheld any one of you from him. (Sura 69:43–47)

A Christian might compare the plural pronouns in the suras above to the Trinitarian concept shown in Genesis 1:26: "Then God said, 'Let Us make man in Our image.'" Some Muslim scholars will debate this point by saying that the "We/Us" pronouns found in many places in the Koran are referring to the idea of a royal or majestic term, like a king saying, "*We* decree the following. . ." The king is not more than one, but he uses a plural form.[197] While this argument might sound convincing at first, neither the Koran nor the Bible explains the use of these terms in this perspective. A Christian can simply ask, "On what authority do you make that claim? If the Koran is from God, then every word in it is significant and may have much deeper meaning." The scholar and evangelist to Muslims, St. Clair W. Tisdall, used that argument while conversing with a Muslim scholar.[198] In fact, it could be argued that the use of the plural form in the Koran is a *sign* to those who read it and that there is a much deeper revelation about the nature of God that should be investigated.

Second, many Islamic scholars over the generations have claimed that the plural is used because Allah is magnanimously including others (for example, Gabriel, other angels, or people) in these ex-

---

197 "Why Does Koran Say 'We and He'?"; www.godallah.com (accessed on April 4, 2016).
198 Sam Shamoun, "The Quran, Allah and Plurality Issues"; anwering-islam.org (accessed April 4, 2016).

pressions. So, then, there is a difference of interpretation by Islamic scholars. Who is right, and by what authority do they claim that their particular interpretation is the correct one?

Conversely, the plural terms used in the Koran could be said to agree with the Bible in places like Genesis 3:22 and 11:7 to teach the doctrine of the Trinity in unity. If a Muslim asks a Christian by what authority he says that the doctrines of the Trinity and the deity of Christ are true, there are numerous biblical passages that can be used to begin such a discussion. Here are a few regarding the Trinity: Genesis 18:1–3, Psalm 110:1, Zechariah 12:10–11, Matthew 3:16–17, John 14:9, Acts 5:3–5, and Hebrews chapters 1–3. Here are a few regarding the deity of Christ: John 1:1, 14, John 8:58, John 20:28, Titus 2:13, 2 Peter 2:1, and Romans 9:5.

Jihad in the Koran

In his book, *Seven Doors to Islam*, author John Renard explains the orthodox views of the *greater* and *lesser* jihads. The fight within oneself is the greater struggle, and the fight against outward foes is the lesser battle. Accordingly, the lesser and greater jihad work hand in hand.

Islamic traditions teach that the lesser jihad fulfills the divine charge of accountability for the shape of society and the world. These "outside" battles might include human rights, environmental issues, or even electing the local school board. The jihad of the sword is permitted, but only as a last resort.[199] Allegedly, it should not include terrorism, mistreatment of prisoners, or the unjustifiable destruction of natural resources.

Today, some Muslims cite verses like the following to justify their view that Islam is essentially peaceful:

> Fight in God's cause against those who fight you, but do not overstep the limits: God does not love those who overstep the limits. Kill them whenever you encounter them, and drive them out from where they drove you out, for persecution is more serious than killing. Do not fight them at the Sacred Mosque unless they fight

---

199 John Renard, 11–13.

you there. If they do fight you, kill them—this is what such disbelievers deserve—but if they do stop, then God is most forgiving and merciful. Fight them until there is no more persecution, and worship is devoted to God. If they cease hostilities, there can be no [further] hostility, except toward aggressors. (Sura 2:190–193, Haleem)

However, history shows that Islam stormed North Africa, Europe, and Asia without being invaded first. John Kelsay explains in his book, *Islam and War: A Study in Comparative Ethics*, that seventh-century Sunni theorists saw the jihad as the "struggle to extend the boundaries of the territory of Islam." Thus, a just cause was found—or created. Lethal force was justified if non-Islamic political entities refused to pay tribute, which was the same as denying the authority of the Islamic state.[200]

Muhammad's seventh-century vision statement can be found in Sura 2:286: "Give us victory over the infidel nations." Militant Islam has plenty of Koranic verses to back up their aggressive view of the jihad. Even moderate leaders often use both aspects of the jihad's meanings to play to the crowds. Viorst wrote, "Some Muslim leaders use whatever definition suits their immediate fancy. It is not unknown for militant Arab leaders to urge foreigners to accept its [jihad's] specific meaning, while gratifying followers at home by proclaiming an allegiance to the armed struggle."[201]

Below are some of the many jihad-of-the-sword verses that modern Islamic militants use to justify their actions. Note that the word *infidel* can refer to Jews, Christians, or any other "unbelievers."

Urging War with the Infidels

Infidels now are they who say, "Verily God is the Messiah Ibn Maryam (son of Mary)!" (Sura 5:19)

Make war upon such of those to whom the Scriptures have been given as believe not in God [Allah]. (Sura 9:29)

Believers! Wage war against such of the infidels as are your

---

200 John Kelsay, *Islam and War: A Study in Comparative Ethics* (Louisville, KY: Westminster/John Knox Press, 1993), 34–35.
201 Viorst, 100.

neighbors, and let them find you rigorous: and know that God is with those who fear him. (Sura 9:124)

Give not way to the infidels, but by means of this Koran strive against them with a mighty strife. (Sura 25:54)

When ye encounter the infidels, strike off their heads till ye have made a great slaughter among them, and of the rest make fast the fetters. (Sura 47:4)

Forbidding Friendships with Infidels

If they turn back, then seize them, and slay them wherever ye find them; but take none of them as friends and helpers. (Sura 4:91)

Verily, the infidels are your undoubted enemies. (Sura 4:102)

O Believers! Take not the Jews or Christians as friends. They are but one another's friends. If any one of you taketh them for his friends, he surely is one of them! God will not guide the evil doers. (Sura 5:56)

But God forbids you to take as allies those who have fought against you for your faith, driven you out of your homes, and helped others to drive you out: any of you who take them as allies will truly be wrongdoers. (Sura 60:9, Haleem)

Teaching Intolerance for People's Religious Views

When the [four] forbidden months are over, wherever you encounter the idolaters, kill them, besiege them, wait for them at every lookout post; but if they repent, maintain the prayer, and pay the prescribed alms, let them go on their way, for God is most forgiving and merciful. (Sura 9:5, Haleem)

Invite not the infidels to peace when ye have the upper hand: for God is with you, and will not defraud you of the recompense of your works. (Sura 47:37)

O Prophet! Make war on the infidels and hypocrites, and deal rigorously with them. Hell shall be their abode! And wretched the passage to it! (Sura 66:9)

Provoking His Men to Fight

When fighting was ordained for them, some of them feared men as much as, or even more than, they feared God, saying,

135

"Lord, why have You ordained fighting for us? If only You would give us just a little more time." Say to them, "Little is the enjoyment in this world and Hereafter is far better for those who are mindful of God: you will not be wronged by as much as the fibre in a date stone." (Sura 4:79, Haleem)

What will you not fight against those Meccans who have broken their oaths and aimed to expel your Apostle, and attacked you first? Will ye dread them? God is more worthy of your fear, if ye are believers! So make war on them: By your hands will God chastise them. (Sura 9:13–14)

Promising Allah's reward for Those Who Fight

Whoever fighteth on God's path, whether he be slain or conquer, we will in the end give him a great reward. (Sura 4:76)

God hath assigned to those who contend earnestly with their persons and with their substance, a rank above those who sit at home. (Sura 4:96)

Accountability: The Koran versus the Bible

Muhammad was accountable to no one for his subjective revelations. Questioning his authority might have resulted in death or military reprisal. It is sad to see that Muhammad was eventually so self-deceived in his own fable and fantasy. He should have listened to his own suras:

Let not this present life then deceive you; neither let the deceiver deceive you concerning God. (Sura 31:38)

For the Satans will turn men aside from the Way, who yet shall deem themselves rightly guided. (Sura 43:36)

Compare the Koran's lack of accountability to the incredible amount of accountability that the Bible offers. Over forty authors wrote the Bible throughout a period of sixteen hundred years. Yet the divine revelation coincides accurately and succinctly with itself. From beginning to end, the Bible builds coherently upon a central, understandable theme.

1. God in the Garden of Eden created Adam and Eve and tested their obedience.
2. They failed, sinned, and death entered the world.
3. God, through His mercy, fashioned a plan of redemption.
4. God worked through Noah, Abraham, Isaac, Moses, David, and others to form a people—the Hebrews—who would faithfully record His words and establish His ways in the world.
5. He promised to them the Messiah, the Great Redeemer! (Isaiah 53).
6. Jesus Christ came as the Messiah, announcing that He was the Son of the Living God (Matthew 16:13–18).
7. He referred to God as His Father.
8. His earthly mission was to teach people about the way of redemption back into the grace of God. That way was through Him and no other! (John 14:6).
9. He proved His authority by numerous recorded miracles.
10. He then died on the cross for people's sins and rose from the dead on the third day, thus fulfilling the many prophecies about Him in the Old Testament.
11. After instructing His disciples, He ascended into heaven before many witnesses.
12. He will return someday for all those who place their faith and trust in Him alone for salvation.

The Bible begins with the account of a garden and men, and it ends with the redemption of men standing before God in His garden.

The Bible obviously impressed Muhammad. Major portions of the Koran are simply supportive statements about the lives of biblical characters and many of their deeds. However, Muhammad often alters events and the presentation of biblical individuals to his own distorted worldview. To him, Jesus could not be God or the Son of God, because that would confound Muhammad's theological philosophy and his own personal claim to be the seal of the prophets—the greatest and the last.

PART FOUR

WRESTLING AGAINST

PRINCIPALITIES AND POWERS

CHAPTER 8

Name Above All Names

Jesus is a master of love; Mahomet is a master of hatred.[202]

—Robert Redeker

A Story of Healing

Although issues about the Koran's validity have been discussed, it should be noted that some of the text is based upon stories from the Old and New Testaments. Some of these have historical validity. For instance, Jesus is portrayed in the Koran as one who can heal. God can use this truth—even in a book like the Koran—to draw people to the Lord Jesus Christ. Once they have given their lives to Him, He can then reveal the truth of the Bible, the true Word of God.

Gulshan Esther had such an experience. Her story, told in *The Torn Veil*, took place in Punjab, Pakistan, in the 1960s and 1970s. She was the youngest daughter of a Shiite Muslim Sayed family that descended directly from the prophet Muhammad.

At six months of age, Gulshan contracted typhoid and became completely paralyzed in half of her body. Soon afterward, her mother died. Gulshan's siblings and relatives lovingly cared for her, especially her father, who never remarried. He prayed for her healing constantly. They traveled to London to find the best doctors, and

---

202 Robert Redeker, "*Face aux intimidations islamistes, que doit faire le monde libre?*" *Le Figaro*, (September 2006).

they even went on a *haj* to Mecca to kiss the Black Stone and ask Allah for healing. Nothing worked.

When Gulshan was a teenager, her father died. Gulshan was heartsick at the loss—and now she was a lonely, crippled orphan. The prayer beads and the Koran that had been so important to her in the past no longer brought her peace. God seemed distant. She despised being a burden to others. Her emotional pain grew, until suicide became an easy choice, but she lacked the mobility or means to carry it out. Tears flowed, and for the first time in her life she asked God openly for help. Amazed, she heard these words: "*I am Jesus, son of Mary. Read about me in the Koran.*"

Gulshan conversed with Jesus and read about Him in the Koran. Several years later, she cried out again. This time, she was crying for the Jesus of the Koran to heal her. In a vision, Jesus commanded her to get up and walk.

She did.

He said, "I am Jesus. I am Immanuel. I am the Way, the Truth, and the Life. I am alive, and I am soon coming. See, from today you are My witness."[203] Then He taught her the Lord's Prayer. She got ahold of a Bible and made a confession of Christ as her Savior.

Gulshan's story exploded in her community, and she gave all the glory to Jesus. Eventually, people pressured her to stop talking so much about Jesus, but she could not. Gulshan, a direct descendant of Muhammad himself, became a missionary for the Lord!

I came to know about Gulshan's amazing testimony from her book, but then in January 2002, I met a couple in Mississauga, Canada, who had once talked with Gulshan herself. They explained to me about an interesting conversation they had had with Gulshan. While talking with her, they were surprised to notice that one of her fingers was still crippled. Why hadn't it been healed with the rest of her body? they wondered. So they asked. And Gulshan informed them that Jesus had left her with one crippled finger to remind her of the great miracle that He had done for her.

---

203 Gulshan Esther, *The Torn Veil* (Fort Washington, PA: Christian Literature Crusade, 1998), 61.

Jesus Christ: Healer and Miracle Worker

What did Gulshan learn about Jesus in the Koran? In the Arabic Koran, Jesus (*Isa*) is referred to over thirty times. Readers are introduced to a more limited and distorted Jesus than the true Jesus who may be found in the Bible, but that is due to the setting in which the Koran was written.[204] Muhammad's information concerning Jesus was restricted. There was no Arabic translation of the Bible, and so accurate biblical information was hard to come by, especially in the days before the printing press. Apparently, Waraqa ibn-Nawfal, the cousin of Muhammad's wife Khadijah, was a Christian, and he might have recited the oral traditions that he had heard from the incomplete version of the Bible that existed in the Syriac language.

In those days, only clerics and monks had a scholarly knowledge of Christianity. Thus, many of the Christian Arabs were not well-versed in truth or orthodoxy. They swayed in their views toward the Monophysites or the Nestorians. The Monophysites leaned heavily on Christ's divinity, but at the expense of His humanity.

The Nestorians were a reaction to and a direct contradiction of the Monophysites. They held that within the incarnate Christ were two separate persons: one divine and one human.[205] His perfect obedience overcame the devil, and His perfect service was a role model of humility for all of mankind to follow.

One other group of Christians might have influenced Muhammad's writing of the Koran. Theologian Hans Küng has suggested that a small group of Messianic Jews existed at that time in Mecca, although they did not regard Jesus to be divine.[206]

The Koran doesn't say much about the attributes of Jesus. However, it says enough for those who are searching—genuinely probing—for the truth, to see that Jesus Christ was unlike any other man who ever lived, including Muhammad. Consider the following suras:

---

204 See Geoffrey Parrinder for a complete listing; *Jesus in the Qur'an* (New York, NY: Oxford University Press, 1977), 18–20.
205 *The Oxford Dictionary of World Religions*, 692.
206 Hans Küng, et al., *Christianity and the World Religions: Paths to Dialogue with Islam, Hinduism, and Buddhism* (London: Collins, 1986).

. . . to Jesus, son of Mary, gave we clear proofs of his mission, and strengthened him by the Holy Spirit. (Sura 2:81)

Out of clay will I [Isa] make for you, as it were, the figure of a bird: and I will breathe into it, and it shall become, by God's leave, a bird. And I will heal the blind, and the leper; and by God's leave will I quicken the dead. (Sura 3:43)

And she made a sign to them, pointing toward the babe. They said, "How shall we speak with him who is in the cradle, an infant?" It [Isa] said, "Verily, I am the servant of God; He [Allah] hath given me the Book, and He hath made me a prophet." (Sura 19:30–31)

And when the Son of Mary was set forth as an instance of divine power, lo! Thy people cried out for joy thereat. (Sura 43:57)

In these verses, we can see that, in the Koran, Jesus had a specific mission. He was strengthened by the Holy Spirit and He displayed divine power. Five special miracles are recorded in the Koran as examples of His divine power:

1. He healed the blind.
2. He healed the lepers.
3. He quickened (raised) the dead.
4. He created a bird from clay and breathed life into it.
5. He spoke from the cradle as a babe.

The first three miracles are validated in the Bible. The fourth and fifth are not. It is unlikely that Jesus was able to speak from the cradle. And whether Jesus actually created a bird from clay is debatable, but the information about this story probably came to Muhammad through an apocryphal book entitled the Gospel of Thomas.[207] It is interesting that the bird miracle could be said to resemble the Genesis account of God creating man and breathing life into him (see Genesis 2:7).

The first three miracles, as I mentioned, are in the Bible, and they help to define the greatness of Jesus' divine power. No healing was impossible; even the dead were raised. The Christian New Testament records numerous eyewitness accounts of Jesus' miracles, in-

---

207 Rodwell, note in *The Koran*, 438.

cluding His stopping the wind and the waves in a storm, casting out demons, walking on water, and turning water into wine. As mentioned in the Koran, His miracles produced great joy in the people.

There are other miracles in the Koran that are associated with Jesus. Sura 5:12–15 relays the miracle of Jesus asking God to send down a feast from heaven. This passage in the Koran can be used by Christians to introduce Muslims to the miracle of Jesus feeding the five thousand people from just a few fishes and loaves of bread, or the feeding of the four thousand in a different passage of the New Testament. Sura 3:49 states: "I will tell you what you may eat and what you may store up in your houses" (Haleem).[208] This sura is often used by Muslims to say that Jesus had foreknowledge beyond that of an ordinary human. He knew what people had eaten or what was in their homes. There are other legendary miracles that Islamic teachers may attribute to Jesus that are not described in the Koran.

Sura 42:11 speaks of having faith. For Christians, this means having a firm trust and belief in Jesus Christ for everything. Sura 33:7 tells of the covenant that Allah made with Isa. For followers of Isa, this is the New Covenant, the New Testament, or the Injil.

Jesus Christ: Sign from God

Some of the apostles we have endowed more highly than others: Those to whom God hath spoken, He hath raised to the loftiest grade, and to Jesus the Son of Mary we gave manifest signs, and we strengthened him with the Holy Spirit. (Sura 2:254)

Mention in the Scripture the story of Mary. She withdrew from family to a place east and secluded herself away; We sent Our Spirit to appear before her in the form of a normal human. She said, "I seek the Lord of Mercy's protection against you: if you have any fear of Him [do not approach]!" but he said, "I am but a Messenger from your Lord, [come] to announce to you the gift of a pure son." She said, "How can I have a son when no man has touched me? I have not been unchaste," and he said, "This is what your Lord said, 'It is easy for Me—We shall make him a sign to all people, a blessing from Us.'" And so it was ordained: She conceived him. (Sura 19:16–22, Haleem)

208 The Qur'an, 38.

We breathed our spirit, and made her and her son a sign to all creatures. (Sura 21:91)
And we appointed the Son of Mary, and His mother for a sign. (Sura 23:52)

Part of Jesus' divine mission was to be a sign. According to the Koran, Allah sent his *spirit* and created a holy son as a sign for mankind. When Christians read this, it reminds us of Luke 1, in which the angel Gabriel announced to Mary that she would conceive a Son who was to be named Jesus, "the Son of the Highest" (Luke 1:32 NKJV). Mary did not understand how she, as a virgin, could have a child.

And the angel answered and said to her, "The Holy Spirit will come upon you, and the power of the Highest will overshadow you; therefore, also, that Holy One who is to be born will be called the Son of God." (Injil, Luke 1:35 NKJV)

The event took place and was recorded six hundred years prior to Muhammad's time on this earth. So, for Christians, the matter is simple—Jesus was given birth by the Holy Spirit through the Virgin Mary, and He is the Holy One, the Son of God. However, in the Koran, Jesus is presented as the son of Mary and not as the Son of God. To Muslims, it is blasphemy to associate Allah's divine nature with the human nature. The Arabic word *shirk* indicates the sin of associating something or someone (i.e., Jesus) with God *as God*. This is the worst possible sin in Islam.[209] Jesus, then, can only be a created being. In Sura 3, He is compared to Adam, as one of the only two prophets who were "born" without natural fathers.[210]

Once again, there are textual problems with the Koran. Gabriel fills the position of the Holy Spirit, and some believe that he is a part of the "We" that refers to Allah. The angel is represented as a normal man. His answer, that he may bestow on Mary a pure son, raises the question of whether or not that was to be accomplished through any carnal action. In reality, according to the Old and New Testaments,

---

209 *The Oxford Dictionary of World Religions*, 883.
210 George W. Braswell Jr., *Islam: Its Prophet, Peoples, Politics and Power* (Nashville, TN: Broadman and Holman Publishers, 1996), 279.

the virgin birth was prophesied and recorded long before the time of Mary, by the prophet Isaiah, who also referred to the Son's divinity:

> Therefore the Lord Himself will give you a sign: Behold, the virgin shall conceive and bear a Son, and shall call His name Immanuel (meaning God with us). (Suhuf-un Nabiyin, Isaiah 7:14 NKJV)

In 1947, a wandering Bedouin goat herdsman explored a cave in the side of the cliffs west of the Dead Sea. He found approximately forty thousand fragments of papyrus from Old Testament books and other ancient literature preserved there. This was called the greatest archaeological discovery of the twentieth century. A complete book of Isaiah was found that dates to at least BC 125. It had been recorded from earlier manuscripts of the same book, and its authenticity is beyond dispute. It bears witness to the sign of the virgin bearing a Son who would be "God with us."[211] Furthermore, Isaiah prophesied about the unique divine attributes of Jesus that were not portrayed in the Koran. Jesus has a name that cannot be matched by any other:

> For unto us a Child is born, unto to us a Son is given; and the government will be upon His shoulder. And His name will be called Wonderful, Counselor, Mighty God, Everlasting Father, Prince of Peace. Of the increase of His government and peace there will be no end, upon the throne of David and over His kingdom, to order it and establish it with judgment and justice from that time forward, even forever. The zeal of the LORD of hosts will perform this. (Isaiah 9:6–7 NKJV)

Jesus Christ: Messiah

> Remember when the angel said, "O Mary! Verily God announceth to thee the Word from Him: His name shall be, Messiah Jesus the son of Mary, illustrious in this world, and in the next, and one of those who have near access to God; and He shall speak

---

211 S. F. Fleming, *Gate Breakers: Answering Cults and World Religions with Prayer, Love and Witnessing* (Seattle, WA: Selah Publishing, 1998), 34. In this book, I spend a chapter discussing the authenticity of the Old and New Testaments.

to men alike when in the cradle and when grown up; and he shall be one of the just." (Sura 3:40–41)

The Koran ascribes the title of "Messiah" to Jesus eleven times, but it never defines this honor. The word *messiah* in Hebrew means "the anointed one." *Christ* is the Greek equivalent of the term *Messiah*. So, *Messiah Jesus* and *Christ Jesus* are similar expressions of His title. Jesus never used the word *Christ* to refer to Himself, but He commended Peter for recognizing it (Matthew 16:16–17), and He admitted to being the Christ, the Son of God, at His trial (Matthew 26:63–64).[212]

For Muhammad, however, Jesus was an apostle, but not the Savior. For Christians and many Jews, the Messiah is the Savior of mankind. The Greek name *Jesus*, or its Hebrew equivalent, *Yeshua*, means "savior." The angel told Joseph that Jesus was given that name because He would "save His people from their sins" (Matthew 1:21 NKJV). John the Baptist said of Jesus, "Behold! The Lamb of God who takes away the sin of the world!" (John 1:29 NKJV).

Jesus Christ: Word of God

The Messiah, Jesus, son of Mary, is only an apostle of God, and his Word which he conveyed into Mary, and a Spirit proceeding from himself. (Sura 4:169)

This sura is partially true, and it confirms a major biblical revelation: Jesus is much more than simply *an apostle*, but He did come as the living Word of God. It is also amazing that Jesus is represented in Islam as Allah's Spirit. Jesus, then, is Allah's *Word* and Allah's *Spirit*. And as seen earlier, He is also the Messiah. No other prophet in the Koran has this description—not even Muhammad himself!

Christians do not deny the Koranic exhortation that there is only one God. Christians agree—and Christianity is a monotheistic religion. Injil, Mark 12:32 proclaims, "There is one God, and there is no other but He" (NKJV). The central teaching of Christianity is that Jesus Christ *is* God! The orthodox doctrine of the Trinity coincides

---

212 Braswell, 279.

with this. When Muslims truly understand what Christians mean by the Trinity, they then realize that Christians also believe in only one God.

As we saw earlier, the doctrine of the Trinity states that within the nature of the one God, there are three eternal Persons: God the Father, God the Son, and God the Holy Spirit. Jesus sent His disciples to all nations and told them to make disciples and baptize "in the name of the Father and of the Son and of the Holy Spirit" (Injil, Matthew 28:19 NKJV). Jesus is the Creator of all that exists; He is not a created being. He defined Himself in the Word of God.

In his book *Al-Masih: The Anointed One*, author Noor ul Haq explains:

> As Word of Allah (*kalimatullah*), Al-Masih Isa was the direct revelation of Allah's will for mankind. In the days of the ancient prophets, Allah revealed His will through the Word of the Holy Books. Now He had revealed His will through the Word of a living human being named Al-Masih Isa.[213]
>
> In the beginning was the Word, and the Word was with God, and the Word was God. (Injil, John 1:1 NKJV)
>
> And the Word became flesh and dwelt among us, and we beheld His glory, the glory as of the only begotten of the Father, full of grace and truth. (Injil, John 1:14 NKJV)
>
> He was clothed with a robe dipped in blood, and His name is called The Word of God. (Injil, Revelation 19:13 NKJV)

It is interesting that Muslims believe each verse of the Koran is a written sign. The Word of God—that is, the Messiah Jesus—came as the incomparable sign of God and He revealed God in the flesh. Muslims believe that the Koran is the perfect tablet that came down from heaven. In truth, Jesus Christ is the "perfect tablet" that came down from heaven, as revealed in the Bible. Interestingly, God did not speak every word that was recorded in the Bible, as Muslims believe of the Koran. Some of the words are transcripts of conversations of men or of demons; others are lists of historical facts. Still, every bit of the text is consistent and unified in its purpose: to reveal God's message of love and salvation.

---

213 Noor ul Haq, *Al-Masih: The Anointed One* (Minneapolis, MN: Center for Ministry to Muslims, 1996), 26.

Author David Hubbard says it well in his book, *Does the Bible Really Work?*

> It says exactly what God wants it to say, and every part of it is important. But one thing more needs to be said, briefly, the Bible is the Word of God. In other words, the Bible's inspiration is permanent, part of its very nature. It does not depend on how we feel about it. The Bible's inspiration is not its ability to turn me on but the fact that God has breathed His own truth in all its sentences and words.[214]

Jesus Christ: Merciful One

> She said: "How shall I have a son, when man hath never touched me? And I am not unchaste." He said: "So shall it be. Thy Lord hath said: 'Easy is this with me;' and we will make him a sign to mankind, and a mercy from us. For it is a thing decreed." And she conceived him. (Sura 19:20–22)
>
> We caused Jesus the son of Mary to follow them; and we gave him the Evangel [gospel], and we put into the hearts of those who followed him kindness and compassion. (Sura 57:27)

Here, motive is added to the mission of Jesus: "a mercy from us [Allah]." Author Noor ul Haq, in his thoughtful booklet entitled *Mercy of Allah*, says that Jesus "was the outstretched hand of Allah. He was the living expression and the personification of Allah's redeeming Mercy."[215] It is interesting that of the ninety-nine names that the Koran has for Allah, *al-Rahman* (Allah, the Merciful, the Compassionate) is found 169 times. *Al-Rahman* was one of the popular monotheistic deities in southern Arabia whose attribute was adopted for Allah by Muhammad and then incorporated into the Koran.

The Koran presents Jesus as a sign of God's mercy and compassion. He was given the "Evangel," which was His teaching of the

---

214 David A. Hubbard, *Does the Bible Really Work?* (Waco, TX: Word Books, 1972), 31–32.
215 Noor ul Haq, *The Mercy of Allah* (Minneapolis, MN: Center for Ministry to Muslims, 1996), 7.

Gospel, the Good News of the New Testament. Here is the basic Gospel message:

> For God so loved the world that He gave His only begotten Son, that whoever believes in Him should not perish but have everlasting life. (John 3:16 NKJV)
> Moreover brethren, I declare to you the gospel . . . that Christ died for our sins according to the Scriptures, and that He was buried, and that He rose again the third day according to the Scriptures. (Injil, 1 Corinthians 15:1, 3–4 NKJV)

God the Father loved people so much that He sent His Son, Jesus Christ, to be the Savior of mankind, by dying on the cross for their sins. Isaiah prophesied that Jesus would bear "the sin of many" (Isaiah 53:12 NKJV), but he also said that Jesus would bear our griefs, sorrows, and transgressions, and that "by His stripes we are healed" (53:4–5 NKJV). Those who accept the sacrifice of Al-Masih Isa on their behalf and place their faith in Him will not perish, but have everlasting life.

Jesus Christ: Risen Savior

Jesus did not stay in the grave, but He rose on the third day. Sura 19:34 mentions Jesus being "raised to life," but it does not say when it happened. Of course, Muslims are not taught that Jesus died on the cross; therefore, His resurrection is a moot point.

The following passage has produced much diversity of thought within Islam:

> And for their saying, "Verily, we have slain the Messiah, Jesus the son of Mary, an Apostle of God." Yet they slew him not and they crucified him not, but they had only his likeness. (Sura 4:156)
> And because they disbelieved and uttered a terrible slander against Mary, and said, "We have killed the Messiah, Jesus, son of Mary, the Messenger of God." (They did not kill him, nor did they crucify him, though it was made to appear like that to them; those that disagreed with him are full of doubt, with no knowledge to follow, only supposition: they certainly did not kill him—No! God

151

raised him up to Himself. God is almighty and wise. There is not one of the People of the Book who will not believe in [Jesus] before his death, and on the Day of Resurrection he will be a witness against them.) (Sura 4:156–159, Haleem)

The crucifixion of Al-Masih Isa is one of the most well-documented facts in human history.[216] Muhammad was either misinformed, misunderstood, or had ulterior motives in writing this passage of the Koran. Either way, it sets up Muslim scholars with a real dilemma. Some have tried to explain it away by saying that Jesus hid while one of His companions died in His place. Others believe that God sent angels to protect Jesus, and Judas Iscariot ultimately died in His place. Another tradition says that God carried Jesus back to heaven before the Jews could kill Him.[217]

A Muslim scholar named Mahmoud M. Ayoub suggests that Muhammad was misunderstood. It is his position that the Koran "does not deny the death of Christ. Rather, it challenges human beings who in their folly delude themselves into believing that they could vanquish the divine Word, Jesus Christ the Messenger of God."[218] Another author, Harry Morin, agrees with Ayoub's assessment that the Koran does not deny the crucifixion and death of Jesus: "Most Muslims accept the birth of Jesus and the raising of Jesus into heaven. It should not be so difficult then for them to believe that somewhere in between, Jesus died."[219]

Finally, Muhammad might have denied the crucifixion because he feared receiving a similar treatment if things got out of hand. So, he revealed that the Christians and Jews were simply mistaken. Muhammad did not want to suffer. He did not come to be a savior, and he could not imagine that God would become a man and then suffer for others.

Yet, historical evidence says that it is Muhammad who was mis-

216 Braswell, 282.
217 Braswell, 283.
218 Mahmoud M. Ayoub, "Toward an Islamic Christology," "The Death of Jesus: reality or delusion," lxx, *Muslim World* (1980), 116.
219 Harry Morin, *Responding to Muslims* (Springfield, MO: Center for Ministry to Muslims, 2000), 61.

taken. Jesus most certainly died on the cross, and He did so before many witnesses. He did it in fulfillment of such Old Testament prophetic passages as those found in Psalm 22, Isaiah 53, and Zechariah 12. The actual Gospel (*evangel*), which the Koran ironically says that it confirms, is all about Jesus dying on the cross for our sins. That is the *good news* of what the Gospel is all about! First Corinthians 15:1–4 explains that the Gospel is the death, burial, and resurrection of Jesus Christ, the Lord. It was the resurrected Christ who said to the amazed disciples, "Behold My hands and My feet, that it is I Myself" (Luke 24:39 NKJV). It was the resurrected Christ who showed Thomas the wounds that He had received on the cross. That is why Thomas exclaimed, "my Lord and my God" to Jesus (John 20:27–28 NKJV).

Hundreds of years before Muhammad was born, the early Church fathers knew that Jesus, the Son of God, had died on the cross, and they spoke out from their time to all those who would come after them about the truth of the cross. Consider the following:

Clement of Rome (CE 96)

> Let us look steadfastly to the blood of Christ, and see how precious that blood is to God which, having been shed for our salvation has set the grace of repentance before the whole world. Let us turn to every age that has passed, and learn that, from generation to generation, the Lord has granted a place of repentance to all such as would be converted unto Him.[220]

Justin Martyr (CE 165)

> We hold our common assembly on the Sun's Day because it is the first day, on which God put to flight darkness and chaos and made the world; and on the same day Jesus Christ our Savior rose from the dead; for they crucified him on the day before Saturn's Day, and on the Sun's Day, which follows Saturn's Day,

---

220 "First Epistle of Clement," chapter 7, *Ante-Nicene Fathers: Volume 9* (Peabody, MA: Hendrickson Publishers, Inc., 2004), 231.

he appeared to his Apostles and disciples and taught them these things, which we have handed on to you for your consideration.[221]

Melito of Sardis (CE 160–177)

Treading upon the earth, yet filling the heaven; appearing as an infant, yet not discarding the eternity of His nature; being invested with a body, yet not circumscribing the unmixed simplicity of His Godhead; being esteemed poor, yet not divested of His riches; needing substance inasmuch as He was man, yet not ceasing to feed the entire world inasmuch as He is God; putting on the likeness of a servant, yet not impairing the likeness of His Father. He sustained every character [belonging to Him] in an immutable nature: He was standing before Pilate, and [at the same time] was sitting with His Father; He was nailed upon the tree, and yet was the Lord of all things. [222]

Tertullian (CE 207)

God lived with men as man that man might be taught to live the divine life; God lived on man's level that man might be able to live on God's level: God was found weak, that man might become most great. If you disdain a God like this, I doubt if you can wholeheartedly believe in a God who was crucified.[223]

Jesus Christ: Name Above All Names

And being found in appearance as a man, He humbled Himself and became obedient to the point of death, even the death of the cross. Therefore God also has highly exalted Him and given Him the name which is above every name, that at the name of Jesus every knee should bow, of those in heaven, and of those on earth, and of those under the earth, and that every tongue should confess that Jesus Christ is Lord, to the glory of God the Father. (Injil, Philippians 2:8–11 NKJV)

221 Justin Martyr, *The Apology*, lxvii, as recorded in Henry Bettenson, *The Early Christian Fathers* (Oxford: Oxford University Press, 1969), 63.
222 Melito, "Discourse of the Cross," *Ante-Nicene Fathers: Volume 8*, 756.
223 Tertullian, *Adversus Marcionem*, ii. 27 as recorded in Henry Bettenson, *The Early Church Fathers* (Oxford: Oxford University Press, 1969), 122.

Jesus (Isa) delivered a crushing blow to Satan (Shaitan) and the demonic *jinn* when He rose from the dead. This process will eventually end with the destruction of Shaitan and his cohorts. Death itself will be cast into the lake of fire. Because Jesus endured the shame of the cross, He has now become the Author and Finisher of people's faith. The Holy Scriptures teach that there is salvation in no other name except for the name of Jesus Christ. Eventually, every knee will bow to Him and confess Him as Lord (Injil, Hebrews 2:14; 4:10; 12:2; Injil, Revelation 20:10; 21:8).

Shaitan and the *jinn* are not yet thrown into the lake of fire. The apostle Paul wrote that Shaitan is trying to blind men's minds to the victory that they can have in Jesus Christ. In the last days, people will turn from the faith and give heed to deceiving *jinn* and their doctrines. Before Al-Masih Isa returns, there will be great deception, hatred, and lawlessness; false prophets will deceive many; nations and kingdoms will war against one another; and there will be famines, pestilences, and earthquakes. His Gospel will be preached as a witness to every nation, and then the end will come (Injil, Matthew 24:4–14; 2 Corinthians 4:4; 1 Timothy 4:1).

There are great battles being waged between the Kingdom of God and the forces of darkness:

> Finally, my brethren, be strong in the Lord and in the power of His might. Put on the whole armor of God, that you may be able to stand against the wiles of the devil. For we do not wrestle against flesh and blood, but against principalities, against powers, against the rulers of the darkness of this age, against spiritual hosts of wickedness in the heavenly places. (Injil, Ephesians 6:10–12 NKJV)

The warfare is spiritual, waged by Christians against the satanic principalities and rulers of the world who attack the lives of people who are without Christ. Spiritual armor is necessary for the spiritual warrior—and the most powerful weapon is prayer.[224]

---

224 In Ephesians 6, Paul explains that the armor of God includes the belt of truth, the breastplate of righteousness, the shoes of the Gospel of peace, the shield of faith, the helmet of salvation, and the sword of the Spirit, which is the Word of God. Associated with this armor is the incessant need for prayer.

CHAPTER 9

Allah Weeps

The pope gets ridiculed every day, but you don't see Catholics organizing terrorist attacks around the world.[225]

—Salman Rushdie

Stories of Surrender

Hassan grew up in an Islamic fundamentalist community. He hated seeing crosses around the necks of his Christian schoolmates. Up until he was a young adult, those children continued to experience this wrath of his through his zealous verbal abuse, his belittlement of their every activity, and even his physical attacks.

One night, however, Hassan dreamed he was wearing his own cross and Muslims were ridiculing him about it. He finally understood a small portion of what Jesus had suffered on the cross. His zeal for persecuting Christians became a zeal for learning about Christ. He located a missionary, got a Bible, and began clarifying his thoughts by writing them down. Six months later, his mother discovered his writings, and his father had Hassan arrested.

Hassan had to leave his country to keep from being killed, but he was so thankful to God for revealing to him the love of Jesus Christ. Hassan became a witness about the peace and truth that he had found in Al-Masih Isa (the Messiah Jesus).[226]

---

225 Salman Rushdie, quoted in "Islam: I don't like the word *Islamophobia*" (October 2, 2012): webcitian.org.
226 Jeff Taylor, "I Must Get a Bible," *Charisma* (October 1997), 53.

By reading the Bible, Hassan discovered that Al-Masih Isa wept over Jerusalem. Jesus knew that the Jews would reject the peace and truth found only in Him, and He also knew the city would be destroyed as a result (Luke 19:41–44).

Today, Allah must be heartbroken over the warring Islamic spirit that incurs great harm in His name. He must weep for Muslims who forsake the peace and truth found only in Jesus.

For those who might think that there is no hope for the Middle East, consider the story of Walid. Like most Muslims, he was taught to hate the Jews. Raised in Bethlehem and Jericho in the 1960s in a Muslim home, Walid saw the conflict and wars going on between Jews and Muslims up close. The first song he ever learned in school was entitled "Arabs Our Beloved, and Jews Our Dogs." As a teenager, he promoted the *intifada* by rioting and throwing Molotov cocktails at the Israeli army. Walid said he was angry at Hitler because he didn't finish the job of eradicating the Jews.

Walid's mother was American, but his father was a Palestinian teacher of English and Islamic Studies. After moving to the United States to receive a college education, Walid's mother converted to Christianity and became convinced of the Bible's accuracy. Walid read a Christian book about the end times and became intrigued about Jesus. In his comparison between the Bible and the Koran, he used the Dead Sea Scrolls to help him eventually conclude that the Bible was accurate and the Koran was not. Finally, Walid prayed for revelation and he came to know Jesus Christ. It amazed him that this same Jesus was a *Jew* from Bethlehem. The name *Bethlehem* means "home of the bread." Walid recognized Jesus as the Bread of Life and the One who came to give life to all—including Muslims *and* Jews.

Walid began to proclaim the love that God had for the Jews and he wept for them. He said that he was ready to give his own life for them as his Lord had done. Quite a transformation of character![227]

The Lord will transform the heart of anyone who truly opens themselves up to Jesus. There are no exceptions. He "desires all men to be saved and to come to the knowledge of the truth" (1 Timothy 2:4 NKJV).

---

227 "Walid's Testimony," *Answering Islam*, http://answering-islam.org/Testimonies/walid.html (accessed April 26, 2016).

Consider the story of Abbas Abhari, who discovered the compassion of the Lord Jesus Christ through the tears of a missionary. As a proud Muslim cleric in the town of Damghan, he heard that a Christian missionary, Ivan Wilson, was telling people about Jesus. Abbas decided to illustrate the superiority of Islam by humiliating the missionary in a debate. Mr. Wilson received Abbas kindly, and the friendly debate eventually reached a stalemate when Abbas clung to the usual Muslim responses: "No, Jesus was not God's Son. . . . He did not die on the cross. . . . He foretold the coming of Muhammad. . . . The Christian Scriptures have been corrupted. . . . Christians worship three gods."

Years later in an interview, Abbas explained what finally changed him:

> Mr. Wilson came here, he talked with me and argued with me, but I felt I had overcome him, and I was feeling very proud of myself. Then that man of God felt so sorry for me in my unbelief and pride that he began to weep. His tears did for me what his arguments did not do. They melted my heart, and I believed and became a Christian. Later, I was baptized.[228]

True Christians need to express brokenness and humility when dealing with those of unbelief. One man said, "Real spirituality will express itself in tears when souls are erring into destruction."[229] Likewise, Jesus wept over the unbelief of those in Jerusalem. His entire ministry was an intercession for them. The apostle Paul served the Lord with humility and tears (see Acts 20:19), and he wept for the enemies of the cross (see Philippians 3:18).

What is truly important is the attitude of the heart. Some people do not weep very easily, but it is the brokenness in our hearts on behalf of others that is important for them to see.

When the World Trade Center collapsed and thousands died on September 11, 2001, cries went up all over the world on behalf of the victims and their families. Many Christians found themselves

---

228 William Miller, *A Christian Response to Islam* (Phillipsburg, NJ: Presbyterian and Reformed Publishing Company, 1976), 125–126.
229 Wes Daughenbaugh, *The Heart God Hears* (Chelalis, WA: Gospel Net Ministries, 1996), 114.

also praying that the families of the perpetrators would come to know the truth about Jesus, the Messiah.

That is one of the weapons of spiritual warfare: Christians are instructed "not to wrestle against flesh and blood," but to fight against the demonic principalities (Ephesians 6:10–12). The following passages deal with different aspects of Christian warfare:

> For though we walk in the flesh, we do not war according to the flesh. For the weapons of our warfare are not carnal but mighty in God for pulling down strongholds, casting down arguments and every high thing that exalts itself against the knowledge of God, bringing every thought into captivity to the obedience of Christ, and being ready to punish all disobedience when your obedience is fulfilled. (2 Corinthians 10:3–6 NKJV)
>
> He who kills with the sword must be killed with the sword. Here is the patience and the faith of the saints. (Revelation 13:10 NKJV)

Islam, Judaism, and Christianity: The Differences

Secular writers, sociologists, and historians may look thoughtfully at the outward appearance of Islam, Christianity, and Judaism, but unless they get to the "spirit" of the matter, they will miss out on the spiritual forces behind these religions. For instance, in comparing the spiritual worldview of these three, do you know which one includes written directives for arms and a physical war to advance and promote their religion?

In Islam, Muhammad killed men. He preached and lived the practice of *jihad*. His successors, the caliphs, took up the principle of coercion and wielded their swords to extend Islam to all the neighboring nations. The Koran embraces the violence, arms, and coercion that modern Muslims use to justify the spread of its message to the entire world. Verses used to defend the Koran as a book of peace are easily countered by other, more fundamentalist verses. Allowing warfare to continue unchecked is a breeding ground for demonic activity.

RELIGION	SCRIPTURE	PERMISSION TO USE ARMS	CONQUEST AND GOAL
Islam	Koran	Yes	Global domination
Judaism	Old Testament	Yes	Israel and its territories
Christianity	New Testament (and OT)	No	Global evangelization

In Judaism, Moses killed an Egyptian when he was young. Later, God used him to miraculously lead the Hebrews out of Egypt and through the wilderness. This included warfare against imposing nations—the Canaanites, the Philistines, and others—to conquer the lands that had been promised to His people by God. Deuteronomy 30:3–6 speaks prophetically of the Jews regaining Israel. The Old Testament embraces but limits the aggressiveness of Jews to the defense or capture of their territories.

In Christianity, however, Jesus lived a life of perfect peace, truth, and love. He taught us that our greatest commandment is to love God and others. He miraculously ministered to other people's needs, even to die on the cross for anyone who would receive His offer of eternal life. He was the ultimate picture of selflessness and sacrifice. After He rose from the dead, He commissioned His disciples to live their lives in the same way and to take the Gospel message into the entire world. Of those disciples whom Jesus commissioned, all but John the Apostle were martyred in foreign lands while peacefully preaching the Good News.[230] The New Testament does not embrace

---

230 John Foxe, *Foxe's Book of Martyrs* (Springfield, PA: Whitaker House, 1891). In chapter 1, Foxe gives an account of all of the first disciples and their consequent deaths as martyrs.

161

violence, arms, or coercion to spread its message. Any use of those means by modern Christians to spread the faith is strictly their own doing, not an edict from Jesus Christ..

Violence and Christianity

The Koran is a document that blinds the minds and hearts of Muslims, thwarting even their best efforts for peace. The limited moral fiber in the book has chained social fairness, immobilized the quest for truth, and unleashed a relentless sword.

Secular commentators have tried to include Christianity in the same category. Certainly, some actions by rogue Christians have been deplorable, justifying violence by taking verses from the Old Testament out of context and interpreting them to support their own agendas. That was not Christ's example. He embraced the Old Testament as a model for inner spiritual principles and truths, but never outward physical violence. Nowhere in the New Testament did He ever command His people to wipe out other nations. On the contrary, Jesus told us to *love* our enemies (see Matthew 5:44). The word *love* appears in the New Testament over 175 times.

It is a mistake to say that Jesus supported violence because of His statements about the sword in Matthew 10:34 and Luke 22:36, in which He asserted that He came to bring a sword and not peace, or when He told His disciples to sell their garments and to buy swords. Once again, in context with the rest of Jesus' words and actions, and those of all of the New Testament authors, those statements have proven to be symbolic. In fact, when facing Roman soldiers, who had orders to take him by force, Jesus healed the man whose ear had been cut off by Peter. Then He reprimanded Peter for that act of violence, by saying, "All who take the sword will perish by the sword" (Matthew 26:52 NKJV). The apostle Paul explains the symbolism of the Christian sword as the Bible, the Word of God (see Ephesians 6:17), which can divide the soul and spirit (see Hebrews 4:12).

What about Christians in the armed forces, however? The answer is that Christian men and women go to battle to defend their countries and to protect their families, not to spread their religion. The Bible can be used to justify conscientious objectors who are morally opposed to fighting, or it can be used to affirm one's responsibility to obey the governing authorities and to fight for one's country (see Romans 13). Clearly, there is no recognizable fundamentalist Christian military, however, marching with orders from the New Testament to ensure that people either turn to Jesus or die.

What about the Catholic-Protestant conflict in Ireland? When the fighting was happening, most Christians in the world believed that it was wrong and that it should stop permanently. They believed they all should live in peace according to the admonition of the New Testament. Still, to clarify further, the fighting in Ireland was being carried out by secular, politicized mobs that were using Christianity as an "attack vehicle." They employed Old Testament contention, rather than justifying their actions through love expressed in the New Testament. In addition, their conflict was *within* Christendom, so to speak. They were not trying to bring Christian law *out to the world* through violence, as is the strategy of Islamic militants with *Sharia* law.

What about fanatical cults? It's easy to find fanatics who abuse religion. In 1977, Jim Jones in Jonestown, Guyana, thought that he had been reincarnated as Buddha, Jesus, and others. He led 914 people into suicide or had them murdered.[231] In 1995, Shoko Asahara, the leader of a Buddhist apocalyptic cult, Aum Shinri Kyo, was responsible for a nerve gas bomb in a Japanese subway station that killed twelve and hospitalized five thousand people.[232] Of course, there are also ultraconservative Christians who have killed abortionists in the name of God. There are White Supremacists who erroneously consider themselves Christians as they continue to terrorize and kill people simply out of racial bigotry. Any reasonable study of their doctrine uncovers a consistent fondness for twisting the Bible, or whatever religious book they employ.

A common White Supremacist doctrine is called the *serpent seed doctrine*. This dangerous invention says that Eve had sex with Satan, thus producing Cain. Later, Satan had sex with Rebekah (Isaac's

---

231 The Watchman Expositor, *2000 Index of Cults and Religions* (Birmingham, AL: Watchman Fellowship, Inc., 2000), Volume 17, No. 1: 28.
232 S. F. Fleming, 8.

wife), producing Esau. Then the claim is that from Esau came all of the darker races, the people "who do not have souls." This deranged doctrine is clearly a distortion of the Old Testament.

Interestingly, the bogus doctrine of the White Supremacists can be easily compared to that of the Alawite branch of modern Islam, a branch that is contrary to mainstream Islam. These adherents believe that *women* do not have souls. The Syrian president, Bashar al-Assad, has embraced this doctrine.[233] When the Koran implies that women are worth less than men, when males receive twice the inheritance of females (Sura 4:12), and when it takes two women to equal the voice of one man in a dispute, it is understandable that a group of extremists like the Alawite branch exists even today.[234]

All religions have extremes, but unfortunately the true warring spirit of the Koran is not held in check by Islam moderates. and it is rarely condemned by mainstream Islam.

Strange Allies

THE NATION OF ISLAM

Within the United States is a group known as the Nation of Islam (the NOI; also called the Black Muslims), but this cultic organization is often rejected by orthodox Islam, which does not want to be identified with it. The group originated back in the 1930s, when an African American named Elijah Poole (Elijah Muhammad) came under the influence of a white man named Wallace D. Fard. The two worked together for a while and drew a following from the African American population. Fard taught that the white man was to be hated because he was the devil, even though Fard was white himself. Eventually, Fard mysteriously disappeared, and Elijah Muhammad took over.

The group has been connected with a modicum of terrorist activity. It was brought under public scrutiny when in February 1965, Malcolm X, one of its former members, was assassinated by a Black

---

233 Andree Seu, "Multi-culti-widowhood," *World Magazine* (September 8, 2001), 53.
234 Weiss, 50.

Muslim death squad for publicly renouncing the teachings of W.D. Fard and Elijah Muhammad. When Elijah Muhammad died in 1975, the group was taken over by Louis Farrakhan in 1977.

Louis Farrakhan has been quite controversial, using racial slurs and anti-Semitic statements. However, he has tried to be somewhat of a champion of African Americans. For example, he organized the Million Man March in Washington, D.C., in which 400,000 to 850,000 African American males marched to promote unity and family values. Many claim that they have been helped by NOI's stance of social reform and its condemnation of drug and gang violence.[235]

That being said, there have been many strange teachings that have cropped up in NOI over the years. Here are a few: Elijah Muhammad taught that Wallace Fard had been the incarnation of Allah. Another teaching said that Fard was the Mahdi. In Sunni Islam, the Mahdi is the successor of Muhammad. Some believe that his coming is to be in conjunction with the Second Coming of Christ. Louis Farrakhan has taught that Allah is a God who appears in human form occasionally, but only as a black man. In fact, white men were supposedly created by a black scientist named Dr. Yakub six thousand years ago, who was living and experimenting in rebellion to Allah.[236] The teachings come from a mixture of Mormonism, Jehovah's Witnesses, New Age, Islam, and even Christianity. Author Robert Morey, in his book *The Islamic Invasion: Confronting the World's Fastest Growing Religion*, points out some of the stranger teachings of NOI with respect to Christianity: Christianity is a white man's religion; Jesus was a black African and only mortal, so there is one temporary god for this world at a time. He promoted the concept of soul sleep, and that Master Elijah Muhammad is currently on a spaceship.[237] In 2010, Farrakhan announced that he was embracing the teachings of the book *Dianetics*, written by L. Ron Hubbard, the founder of Scientology. Since then, NOI has been hosting

235 "Nation of Islam," Wikipedia.org. (accessed September 26, 2016).
236 Eric Pement, "Louis Farrakhan and the Nation of Islam," *Christian Research Institute* (June 9, 2009), equip.org; "Nation of Islam," ibid.
237 Robert Morey, *The Islamic Invasion: Confronting the World's Fastest Growing Religion* (Eugene, OR: Harvest House Publishers, 1992), chapter 11.

its own Scientology auditing courses, and in 2013 it had a graduation ceremony for 8,400 members. That is a significant portion of their members, whom NOI reported as being 20,000 to 50,000 in 2007.[238]

The formal religion of Islam has a lot of theological problems with NOI, as the following explains:

> The Institute for Islamic Information and Education, a Sunni Muslim group in Chicago, contends that the "Nation of Islam" is a misnomer since the NOI denies essential elements of Islam— the most important being that Allah has never appeared in physical form and cannot be identified in that way with any created being. For example, current editions of the NOI's newspaper state, "WE BELIEVE that Allah (God) appeared in the Person of Master W. Fard Muhammad, July 1930."
>
> Orthodox Muslims also believe in a literal, physical resurrection of the dead to heaven or hell, whereas the NOI claims, "No already physically dead person will be in the Hereafter: that is slavery belief, taught to slaves to keep them under control." Instead, Farrakhan teaches that the resurrection of the dead is a *mental* resurrection (understood as an awakening in one's mind from dead thoughts).
>
> Mainstream Muslims also criticize other NOI practices, which include its beliefs about the origin of the races, the NOI's nonobservance of the five daily prayers, and inadequate emphasis on the *hadith* (traditions) of Muhammad and the pilgrimage to Mecca. Farrakhan's recent statements, however, indicate that the NOI is emphasizing some of these areas more strongly.[239]

Chrislam

The syncretism of Christianity and Islam has emerged in the last couple of decades. The term *Chrislam* was coined by author Arthur C. Clark as a futuristic religion in his 1993 book *The Hammer of God*. Yet, there are worship centers in Nigeria and elsewhere that are trying to implement the concept. The leaders of these congregations focus on the similarities of the two religions. Nigeria is a hotbed of

---

238 "Nation of Islam," ibid.
239 Eric Pement, ibid.

animosity and friction between Islam and Christianity. So, there is an attempt to bring peace by allowing worship by both Muslims and Christians in the same place. However, there can never be any equal footing between such diverse worshipers because the focus of their worship is ultimately different. One group is worshiping Allah and believing that the Christians are considered infidels. The other group is worshiping Jesus and believing that the Muslims are confused and lost.

One criticism of Christians who get involved in this *Chrislam* is that they are naïve and will never win out.

> Some misguided Christians believe they can somehow combine the two religions and still have something recognizable as the Christian faith. Sorry, but it can't happen.
>
> Muslims are happy to use such versions of religious syncretism to gain entry into Christian circles, but it just results in the creation of more dhimmitude—Christians becoming second-class citizens.
>
> Islam always wins in such attempts, while Christianity always loses. The truth is, the two religions are fully incompatible. They may seem to be similar (both are world religions, both have Abrahamic origins, both are monotheistic, etc.), but the differences are far greater.
>
> Yet some quite foolish Christians think they can blend their faith with that of Islam and still remain intact, effective, and biblical. Sorry, but it just does not—indeed, cannot—happen.[240]

The Weeping Continues

Women

David Landes, author of *The Wealth and Poverty of Nations*, relates that although some Muslim countries—like Turkey, Egypt, and Iran—have given women the right to vote, they have not shared any real power with the female gender:

> The economic implications of gender discrimination are most

---

240 Bill Muehlenberg, *Culture Watch*, as quoted on belief.net.com (accessed September 26, 2016).

serious. To deny women, is to deprive a country of labor and talent. . . . In general, the best clue to a nation's growth and development potential is the status and role of women. This is the greatest handicap of Muslim Middle Eastern societies today, the flaw that most bars them from modernity. . . . The women are humiliated from birth. The message: Their very existence is a disaster, their body a sin. The boys learn that they can hit their sisters, older and younger, with impunity.[241]

Conversion to Islam is not always voluntary. The Society for the Protection of the Rights of the Child (SPARC) reports that in 2011 that up to two thousand women and girls in Pakistan were forcibly converted and endured rape, kidnapping, and torture.[242]

Women and Sharia

As mentioned previously, women in Muslim countries are not normally given basic equality with men. Here are some examples: In Saudi Arabia, women are not allowed to drive cars on public roads, even though they can be medical doctors, nuclear physicists, or have other professions. Women in Morocco are treated as minors when they apply for certain work-related positions. Though women are allowed to work in Egypt, they are usually restricted from the private sector. Some countries require women to wear full facial burkas or a chador, which opens in the front. Some reports say that as many as five thousand women are murdered each year in what is known as honor killings. These are women who have supposedly broken a Sharia law and are killed by relatives or hostile neighbors.[243]

In a 2011 survey conducted by Trust Law, a legal news service run by the Thomson-Reuters Foundation, the five most dangerous countries for women in the world are Afghanistan, D.R. Congo, Pakistan, India, and Somalia. Of the five, three are dominated by Islam. Afghanistan, Pakistan, and Somalia are countries where the

---

241 Ibid., 412–413.

242 Aliya Mizra, "2,000 minorities girls converted to Islam forcibly: report," *Daily News* (September 5, 2012): webcitation.org.

243 "Muslim Statistics" (Honor Violence), wikiislam.net (accessed September 29, 2016).

majority of the populations are Muslim. According to respondents, the most dangerous country in the world for nonsexual violence is Afghanistan, and for cultural/tribal/religious factors, it is Pakistan[244]

According to ex-Muslim Nonie Darwish, when a wife is beaten by her husband, she has no right to divorce him. Sharia law, which creates legal statutes based on the Koran, gives men more rights. It bears repeating that a woman's testimony in court is only half the value of a man's. A daughter's inheritance is half that of her brother's. A wife cannot leave the house or country without her husband's permission. If a woman gets raped, there must be four witnesses that observe the literal act in order to verify that it was rape; otherwise, the man normally gets off free.

In 2011, three out of four women in prison in Pakistan were there because, as victims of rape, they could not prove that they were innocent. In Sharia law, illicit sex is called *zina*. In order for a woman who is raped to be considered innocent, she must be able to produce four pious male witnesses to verify that she was raped rather that she might have given consent to have sex.[245]

Though not all Islamic countries are as extreme in their Sharia court systems like Saudi Arabia, Pakistan, and Iran, even in moderate countries, like Turkey or Jordan, Sharia law is often carried out unofficially by individual families. So beheadings, stonings, or other forms of honor killings are sometimes carried out by a chosen family member against a woman in that family, and it can be for any number of reasons, such as apostasy. [246]

Female circumcision has become another controversial topic in health organizations and within Islam itself. There are different categories of female circumcision, and the more aggressive procedures are called female genital mutilation (FGM). Getting accurate data about it is difficult because cultures often discourage discussion of

244 "The world's five most dangerous countries for women: A Thomson Reuters Foundation global poll of experts," June 15, 2011, as posted in webcitation.org.
245 Uzma Mazhar ,"Rape, Zina, or Incest: Islamic Perspective," *Muslim Access* (2002); webcitation.org. (accessed September 19, 2016).
246 Michelle A. Vu, "Interview: Ex-Muslim Women on Life under Sharia Law," *The Christian Post* (April 9, 2009); www.christianpost.com (accessed March 31, 2016).

the practice. It is kind of like the *elephant in the living room* that everyone sees, but no one discusses because of embarrassment and awkwardness. However, it is practiced in thirty countries in parts of Africa, Asia, and the Middle East, where at least 125 million women have reported having it done to them.[247] While some adherents of Islam say that the practice is not related to any *requirement* within Islam, others say that it must be done.[248]

The Koran does not address the issue of circumcision for either men or women, and the practice of female circumcision is said to predate Islam, but cultures in modern Islamic societies often practice it and some declare that the *Hadith* supports the practice. While there are Islamic scholars today who dispute the strength (accuracy, intent, and traditional validity) of the particular hadiths used to support the practice, it cannot be denied that the four major Sunni schools of Sharia Law approved of female circumcision (FGM) based on these hadiths and that `Umdat as-Salik's classic manual of Islamic sacred law in the original Arabic language, *Reliance of the Traveler*, said that circumcision was "obligatory" for both men and women.[249]

Slavery

Muslim countries have a problem with modern-day slavery. Slave trafficking was endorsed in Lebanon right up into the 1970s. In the 1960s in Saudi Arabia, fifteen thousand people were being imported every year. In the mid-1980s, Africans were still being tricked into visiting Mecca before being abducted. In his book, *Islam's Black Slaves*, Ronald Segal points out that the only reason Saudi Arabia is not currently trafficking in slavery has been the multitude of temporary Asian settlers. These contract laborers practice a form of servitude that closely resembles slavery, making slavery itself

---

247 Vanja Berggren, "Female Genital Mutilation: Studies on primary and repeat female genital cutting," ibid.

248 "The Truth About Islam and Female Circumcision," *Inside Islam: Dialogues and Debates* (February 18, 2011): insideislam.wisc.edu (accessed April 1, 2016).

249 "Hadiths on Female Circumcision (FGM)," *Unity* (March 19, 2014): unity1. wordpress.com, and "Circumcision," *Answering Islam*, answering-islam.org (accessed April 1, 2016).

seem superfluous.[250]

Today, it is estimated that the Islamic Republic of Mauritania has six hundred thousand slaves, even though slavery is against the law there.[251] According to Christian Solidary International, there are still thirty-five thousand slaves in Sudan.[252] This figure does not include many women and girls, who are taken by soldiers to become their personal sex slaves.[253]

The horror of slavery surely brings tears to many eyes. It is documented that there are slaves trafficked for labor or sex in Afghanistan, Egypt, Indonesia, Mauritania, Pakistan, Saudi Arabia, Sudan, and Yemen.[254] The Islamic State has been accused by the United Nations and various human rights organizations of systematically snatching and raping thousands of women and girls as young as twelve years of age. The stolen girls were given as gifts to Islamic State fighters. Boko Haram kidnapped 276 girls from a Nigerian school. The issue of seizing women to become slaves is so rampant in the Islamic world that Islamic State theologians issued *fatwas* (legal rulings) in 2015, explicitly telling abductors of when they could have sex with the captives.[255]

In chapter 1 of this book you are holding, the story is told of how Gate Breaker Ministries got involved with starting schools in the Punjab region of Pakistan. Some are trade schools for disadvantaged women, and there are other literacy schools for children who are indentured bond servants in brickyards. The Pakistani government does not provide school for these children. The United Nations and many people in Pakistan refer to them as "slaves" because they are not in a normal indentured-bond servant system. Their debt is

250 Ronald Segal, *Islam's Black Slaves* (New York, NY: Farrar, Straus, and Giroux, 2001), 202–203.

251 Nick Meo, "Half a million African slaves are at the heart of Mauritania's presidential election" (July 12, 2009): webcitation.org.

252 "Slavery in Sudan," *Christian Solidarity International*, csi-usa.org.

253 Justin Lynch, "Women Are Sex Slaves in South Sudan's Civil War," *The Daily Beast* (March 13, 2016), the dailybeast.com.

254 "Muslim Statistics" (Slavery), wikiislam.net.

255 Jonathan Landay, Warren Strobel, and Phil Stewart, "Islamic State ruling aims to settle who can have sex with female slaves," CNN (December 29, 2015): truthandgrace.com.

not paid in service after seven years, twenty years, or any amount of years. They fall deeper into financial debt to the brickyards each month, and they must pay off the total amount in order to gain their freedom. Yet, even if they do somehow come up with the money to buy their freedom, they often end up back as slaves in the brickyards, because they are uneducated and they know no other skill.

It is estimated that 1.7 million children in Pakistan are slaves. However, since there are no official statistics, it is impossible to know for sure. These children are forced to work on both farms and in brickyards twelve hours per day, six days per week. The children in GBM schools must also work twelve hours each day, but they are provided education for two to three hours per day in their "time off." There are approximately twenty thousand brickyards in the Punjab region of Pakistan, each with its own slaves.[256]

Hijacking the Mind

David Minor, who was a spiritual mentor of mine, a well-respected apostolic pastor, once defined *stronghold* as "a system of thinking that, if held long enough, becomes easy for demonic powers to reinforce."[257] Consider five points that help define a stronghold.[258]

1. Strongholds are in the Mind.

> Muslims do not challenge their faith in Islam. They are taught to believe and obey. This system prohibits an honest evaluation of those beliefs. They are even taught to target anyone who makes fun of Muhammad or who even draws a cartoon of him.

256 Aliya Mirza, "2,000 minorities girls converted to Islam forcibly: report," *Daily Times* (September 5, 2012): webcitation.org and Muslim Statistics / Slavery at wikiislam.net.
257 David Minor, Sermon at the House of the Lord Church, Oldtown, Idaho (January 14, 1996).
258 Ed Silvoso, *That None Should Perish: How to Reach Entire Cities through Prayer Evangelism* (Ventura, CA: Regal Books, 1994), 158–168.

2. Strongholds can be Based on Good Thoughts.

> Anyone can justify his or her own thoughts—even pious ones. It doesn't mean those thoughts are true.

3. Strongholds often Develop in the Shadow of our Strength.

> Muslims encourage many good deeds and a pious lifestyle that helps to drown the doubts in their minds.

4. Strongholds are often Activated by Trauma.

> Trauma, in this case, could simply be an increase in Islamic terrorism. Muslims are lured into irrational thinking that deludes them to rationalize their fanaticism.

5. Strongholds cause Spiritual and Emotional Instability.

> For Muslims, genuine curiosity is stifled quickly in a quagmire of tradition. The truth is deflected away, as if it were a tempting dart from Satan (Shaitan). The battle of the heart can be twisted and acted out through the guise of jihad. Confused Muslims think they have overcome when, in fact, they have been overcome by a great deception.

The Maze

Finding the right path to truth should be everyone's goal. Unfortunately, many religions and philosophies make it difficult, by creating mazes for people to follow. Corridors lead into different paths, sometimes crisscrossing, sometimes separating into more complex ideologies. To simplify the maze, some people claim that all ways lead to truth—which is truly pure speculation. There is no verifiable evidence to support that view.

Christianity offers something more: a straight path to Jesus Christ by putting our faith in Him. He said, "I am the way, the truth, and the life. No one comes to the Father except through Me" (John 14:6).

It is important for Christians to understand one thing that can be quite confusing for Muslims. Phil Parshall makes an insightful comment in his book *The Cross and the Crescent*. While visiting the town of Midsayap, in Mindanao, Philippines, he noted that on the main street there was one Muslim mosque compared to following churches:

- Four Square Gospel
- Church of Jesus Christ of Latter-Day Saints
- Roman Catholic
- United Church of the Philippines
- Southern Baptist
- Church of the Deliverance
- Christian and Missionary Alliance.[259]

Mature Christians understand the differences in that list as Catholic, mainstream denominations, one independent, and a cult. Yet, what is a Muslim to think? If all Christian cults, sects, denominations, independents, and other meeting places simply called their meeting places *churches*, Muslims would better understand the comparison to *mosque*.

But once converted, Muslims may still wonder how to practice Christianity. There is a lot of variety. From childhood, Muslims are taught strict rituals on exactly how and when to pray, which direction to face, when to attend the mosque, how much to give, what to think, what to wear, and what to say. The ritual practices of Christianity are not nearly so set. People pray when, what, where, and how they want. Church service schedules vary. Also, people worship the Lord in different styles, according to the church they attend. What is the bottom line? Christians have freedom to live for and relate to the Person of Jesus Christ, Al-Masih Isa. The emphasis is not on *how* it is done, but *who* is receiving the worship. A personal, living

---

259 Phil Parshall, *The Cross and the Crescent* (Wheaton, IL: Tyndale House Publishers, 1989), 206.

relationship with the Lord Jesus Christ is what connects Christians, regardless of church affiliation.

The Koran acknowledges that Isa was the Messiah, a prophet, miracle worker, and one who was miraculously born of the Virgin Mary. It also accepts the divine inspiration of the Torah, the Psalms, and the Gospels of Isa (Sura 2:79). Yet, it denies that Isa is the Son of God and that God is the heavenly Father. If Isa was God in the flesh, and Muslims deny Him, then to whom are Muslims actually praying?

The True Way: Al-Masih Isa

Muslims argue that Sharia Law puts them on the right way. Jews say the Torah puts them on the right way. Buddhists teach that they are on the middle way (not worldly, not ascetic); Baha'i and Hindus think that all religions have the right way.

Jesus said that He is the only Way.

Jews and Muslims have a religion based on works: They try to live holy lives based on their scriptural laws. Christianity is based on faith: Believers try to live through Christ's righteousness, accepting forgiveness for their sin and rejoicing in the free gift of salvation that comes through the substitution of Jesus Christ on the cross.

The Bible says that sin separates us from God (Isaiah 59:2) and that all men have sinned (Romans 3:23). God is sovereign and He may extend His grace on Judgment Day to those who tried to live a good life of works by the laws of Judaism and Islam before the Lord (Romans 2:12–16), but why wait? Jesus came to be the hope of everyone. He received the penalty of sin for *all* people who will receive Him. It's as simple as that. You cannot work your way to heaven. Accept Jesus Christ as Lord and Savior. He loves you and desires you to be with Him.

CHAPTER 10

Christian Jihad and True Peace

Prayers open a whole planet to a man's activities. I can as really be touching hearts for God in faraway India or China through prayer, as though I were there. Not in as many ways as though there, but as truly.[260]

—S. D. Gordon

Christian Jihad

Christian Persecution

Persecution against Christians is often underreported by news agencies, possibly because there is simply too much of it. One estimate states that around the world each month, 322 Christians are killed for their faith, 214 churches and Christian properties are destroyed, and 772 forms of violence are committed against Christians. These can include beatings, abductions, rapes, arrests, and forced marriages. Christians in dozens of countries face persecution from their governments or their neighbors because of their faith in Jesus Christ.[261]

The number of Christians who are killed annually for their faith varies. In some years, when nations with significant Christian populations are at war (i.e., Democratic Republic of Congo), the number

---

260 S. D. Gordon, *Quiet Talks on Prayer* (New York, NY: Grosset & Dunlap/Fleming H. Revell, 1941), 15.
261 "Christian Persecution," *Open Doors*, opendoorsusa.org, (accessed September 28, 2016).

increases rapidly. Some statisticians have said that as many as one hundred thousand Christians are being martyred each year. Yet others have challenged that statistic as an annual average, saying that the numbers were inflated. What statisticians do agree upon is that at least seven to ten thousand Christians are killed annually for their faith. This number can drastically increase, depending on what is happening in any particular year.[262]

Though statisticians might disagree in the number of Christians being martyred each year, there is a growing realization that Christianity is the most persecuted religion in the world. David Cameron, the former prime minister of England, has suggested that idea. Pope Benedict XVI mentioned this in 2011. The chancellor of Germany, Angela Merkel, said the same in 2012.[263] According to a Pew Research Report, harassment of Christians by governments and societies rose from 102 countries in 2013 to 108 countries in 2014. Christians are the most persecuted of any religious group around the world.[264] And not surprisingly, in 2011, nine of the top ten persecutors of Christians were Islamic countries.[265]

How to Respond

Emmanuel Chome is a pastor of a church in Lamu, Kenya. He is part of the Kenya College of Ministry, in which I serve as the head of academic affairs. The school was started as a partnership between Capital Christian Center in Meridian, Idaho, and my own ministry, Gate Breaker Ministries. In June 2014, Pastor Emmanuel's community came under attack by al-Shabab, an Islamic terrorist group in Somalia with ties to al-Qaeda. The terrorists sought out the men in the community and asked them if they were Christian. If the men

262 Ruth Alexander, "Are there really 100,000 new martyrs each year?" *BBC News* (November 12, 2013): bbc.com.
263 Nelson Jones, "Are Christians really the world's most persecuted religious group?" *New Statesman* (April 10, 2014): newstatesman.com.
264 Teresa Welsh, "Study: Christians are the most persecuted religious group in the world," *McClatchy DC* (June 27, 2016): mcclatchydc.com.
265 Muslim Statistics (Persecution), wikiislam.net (accessed September 29, 2016).

said, "yes," then they were executed immediately. Dozens of Christian men were killed. Pastor Emmanuel's entire congregation fled the area, except for him and his family. He stayed and continued to serve the Lord. His courage and fortitude impacted the members of the congregation and slowly they began to return. The church actually grew as people recognized the need to stand strong for Christ, even in the midst of trials and tribulation.

The true weapons of Christians are spiritual, not physical; this is a much different manner than how Islam spreads its message. Christian spiritual weapons are *mighty* in God. The word *mighty* is from the Greek word *dunatos*, meaning "powerful" or "capable." This has the same root as the word *dynamite*. The spiritual weapons of God are of greater potency in God's eyes than swords, guns, suicide bombers, or any demonic stronghold. Even though those principalities have bound Islamic rationale in deceit, they cannot ultimately overcome the truth of Jesus Christ. He is the "head of all principality and power" (Colossians 2:10 NKJV). He has been given all authority in heaven and on earth (Matthew 28:18).

Perhaps the Bible has a better handle on true spiritual jihad than even the Koran. A Christian jihad would be "an inner struggle for submission to God combined with an outward resistance that overcomes the devil and his dominion." This is a major part of the Christian calling.

In the late 1980s, David Shibley made an insightful point about the growing openness among Muslims to the Gospel and the arousal to evangelism by Christians who were approaching it in a spiritual militant fashion.

> Millions of Muslims are embarrassed by Islam's more belligerent exponents. This has produced widespread discontent as more and more Muslims search for a true knowledge of God and His ways. While it cannot be said that Muslims are yet turning to Christ in massive numbers, it is true that more seeking Muslims are coming to Christ than ever before. . . . It seems clear that most religions are becoming more militant. Christianity as well is becoming more militant but with an important difference. Our

aggression is motivated by love, not hate. And our arsenal is not material, but spiritual.[266]

The growing openness among Muslims that Shibley referred to in the 1980s has come to pass in Iran. For instance, before the Islamic Revolution of Iran in 1979, only five hundred people confessed to being Muslim converts to Christianity. In a 2000 survey, however, the Christian demographic reported a landslide increase of between four thousand to twenty thousand Muslim converts. This is very significant and is probably not even the total, since many people are afraid to categorically say that they have converted in countries where the reaction can be life-threatening.[267]

The Church may have a golden opportunity to harvest ripe souls, as confused Muslims genuinely critique their own faith.

Three major weapons that Christians have are prayer, love, and witnessing. Through the use of these three weapons, countless people have come to know Jesus Christ as Savior and Lord. Nations and destinies have been changed. These spiritual missiles can bring a new kind of jihad, one that lays bare the faulty ideologies and demonic principalities of Islam.

The Power of Prayer

The great prayer warrior E. M. Bounds once said:

> Prayer is of transcendent importance. Prayer is the mightiest agent to advance God's work. Praying hearts and hands only can do God's work. Prayer succeeds when all else fails. Prayer has won great victories, and rescued, with notable triumph, God's saints when every other hope was gone. Men who know how to pray are the greatest boon God can give to earth—they are the richest gift earth can offer heaven. Men who know how to use this weapon of prayer are God's best soldiers, His mightiest leaders.[268]

266 David Shibley, *A Force in the Earth: The Charismatic Renewal and World Evangelism* (Altamonte Springs, FL: Creation House, 1990), 137.

267 Joel C. Rosenburg, *Inside the Revolution* (Carol Stream, IL: Tyndale House Publishers, 2011), Chapter 25: "The Big Untold Story," Kindle edition.

268 E. M. Bounds, *Purpose in Prayer* (New York, NY: Fleming H. Revell Company, 1920), 79.

We as Christians need to be humble in our prayers for Muslims, because it is not as though we have God, life, or religion all figured out and Muslims have nothing figured out. However, the one thing that we do know and that is of the utmost importance is that Jesus Christ is the Son of the Living God and that He came to die on the cross for our sins and to open the way for us to eternal life. Jesus said, "I am the way, the truth, and the life. No one comes to the Father except through Me" (John 14:6 NKJV). So, our number-one prayer for Muslims is that they would have an encounter with Jesus.

One of the reasons Muslims have been giving their lives to Christ in unprecedented numbers is that Christians are praying for them. Beginning in October of 1993, Christians around the world were challenged to pray for the 10/40 window and one hundred Gateway cities. The 10/40 window is a geographical latitude region encompassing 10 degrees to 40 degrees north of the equator and from western Africa all the way across Asia. Within that region were nearly three billion of the world's least-evangelized people. This movement became the greatest prayer effort in the history of the world up to that time.[269]

Every year, through this organization and others, Christians are challenged to spend time in prayer for Muslims. Some of the results that have been attributed to the prayers for the 10/40 window are as follows: Over forty million Christians interceded with the *Praying Through the Window 6* initiative; in Nigeria, more than one million people gave their lives to Christ in a single service; in 2002, key Christian leaders in India attributed the conversion of hundreds of thousands of Indian Dalits and the planting of thousands of churches to the effectiveness of the prayer movement; in 1989, there were only three known Christians in Mongolia, but by 2003, there were twenty thousand.[270]

For years now the Church has been praying for the people in that region of the world. Prayer has impact, as it rises up like incense before the throne of God. He is able to heal, to secure miracles,

269 *Light the Window* Video, Produced by CBN International, 977 Centerville, Turnpike, Virginia Beach, VA, 23464, 1995.
270 Window International Network, "Prayer Results," win1040.com, (accessed September 12, 2016).

to encourage from a distance, and to thwart demonic plans. Prayer from a humble heart can prevail. For example, in answer to Hezekiah's prayer, an angel slew one hundred eighty-five thousand soldiers of Sennacherib's army in one night (2 Kings 19:35). Is it possible that prayer is dislodging or sorely pricking demonic principalities? Author and speaker George Otis Jr. proposed the idea that at the epicenter of the unreached world stand two powerful demonic forces of great biblical significance: the prince of Persia (Iran) and the spirit of Babylon (Iraq).[271] Both continue to resist the prayers of the saints.

Ed Silvoso makes an interesting claim about Satan. In his book, *That None Should Perish*, he writes, "Once Satan's camp is infiltrated, he will stage a diversionary counterattack by orchestrating weird demonic manifestations."[272] Although Silvoso did not write this in reference to Islam and its terrorist activities, the principle of it is valid. Could rising terrorist activity be the result of angry principalities that are trying to divert our prayers away? Prayer changes people. Prayer changes nations.

Prayer Miracle for Jakarta

As I stood on the top floor of the Istiqlal Mosque, the largest mosque in Southeast Asia, and looked down upon thirty thousand Muslim men praying to Allah during a Friday noon hour in late October 2002, my heart broke for those people.

Just a week earlier, I had been in Japan teaching in Bible schools, when the news of the bombing of a nightclub in Bali, Indonesia, happened. A violent Islamist group named Jemaah Islamiyah was responsible for killing 202 people and injuring many others. Of those killed, eighty-eight were Australians. A message on an audio cassette purportedly from Osama bin Laden declared that the attack was in response to the United States's war on terror and Australia's role in liberating East Timor.[273]

---

271 "Praying Through the Window IV: Light the Window,"AD2000 & Beyond Website. www. Ad2000.org/.
272 Silvoso, 271.
273 Tony Parkinson, "'Bin Laden' voices new threat to Australia," *The Age* (November 14, 2002): theage.com.au.

The plan had been for me to go to Jakarta, Indonesia, after the ministry in Japan, and teach at a Bible school, but after the report of the bombing, we wrestled with the idea of cancelling the trip. Yet when a supernatural peace overtook us about continuing with our plans, we headed for Jakarta. After several days of teaching, I was humbled to be asked to speak at a Bible school graduation on Thursday evening. The Lord told me—a pastor from America, where I could worship freely—to share with the graduates and their families about a *spirit of faith*. Even though I felt like I had nothing to offer these people, who were constantly being persecuted for their faith, the presence of the Lord filled the place, and people wept during the ministry time.

I convinced two of the Indonesian pastors to take me to a mosque on Friday before my flight would leave later that day. Though I had been studying about Islam for years, I had never visited a mosque before. Jakarta at that time had roughly eight to nine million people and thousands of mosques. I had no idea which mosque they were going to take me to, but it took three hours to get to it. When we arrived, I learned that it was called the Istiqlal Mosque and that it was the national mosque of Indonesia. It was an enormous building.

We arrived there at noon as thousands of men were entering for the Friday prayer service. My pastor friends had tried to avoid arriving at that time, but the traffic caused a delay. As I stood on the sidewalk near the sign of the mosque, a "spirit of faith" rose up in me, and I told the pastors that I wanted to look inside the mosque. They did their best to dissuade me, saying that it was dangerous for a westerner like me, but I was determined.

I began making my way to the front door of the mosque. However, I was surrounded by peasant children about two hundred feet from the entrance who were begging for money. Then men from the mosque saw me and came over. Soon I had a number of men and children around me, and the two Indonesian pastors who had accompanied me were trying to extricate me from a potentially volatile situation. I began to think that my plan to look into the front door of the mosque was a mistake.

Then something amazing and wonderful happened. A guard in a green uniform walked up to see what all the ruckus was about. He said to me in English, "What do you want?" I was amazed to hear clearly spoken English after days of everything being interpreted for me. I said to him, "I just want to look into the mosque." He asked, "Why do you want to look inside the mosque?" Now, the pastors had warned me not to tell anyone that I was a pastor. So I said, "I study religion and want to see what it is all about." The guard thought about my request for a moment. Then he said, "Okay, follow me." He invited my friends also.

This man had authority. As we followed him, people moved out of the way. When we entered the mosque, we were instructed to take off our shoes and to wash out feet. Then the guard took us to the barricaded stairwell. He moved the barricade and took us up to the various levels and began to tell me everything that I could absorb about the mosque. The word *Istiqlal* means "independence" in honor of Indonesia's independence. Its capacity is 120,000 people. The large pillars are four stories high. As we got to the top floor and looked down, the guard was kind enough to take our photo on a cheap, disposable camera I had brought. Then he left us for about ten minutes.

Below me were about thirty thousand men participating in *Ju'mah* (congregational noon-prayer on Friday). The women were in a separate room. I took a photo of the men praying below. The noise level up where we were at was deafening as the men below carried out their ritualistic prayer on floormats.

As I gazed down, I thought of my own perilous journey to find truth when I was a young man through drug-mind expansion, philosophy, the occult, wandering through the wilderness, etc., and how the Lord Jesus intercepted me to reveal that He was the Truth. I thought of the verse that had impacted me, Jeremiah 29:13: "You will seek Me and find Me, when you search for Me with all your heart" (NKJV). I prayed, *Surely, Lord, some of these people are seeking You with their whole heart.*

So, I began to pray loudly for salvation for them. I prayed in the Spirit and I prayed with my understanding (1 Corinthians 14:15). It was so loud in there that I was shouting my prayers, jumping up and down in great excitement. Then the two pastors joined me in prayer, and so all three of us were doing it. It was a miraculous, anointed time of praying. After a while, the guard returned, and it was time for me to head to the airport for the long journey home, but the miracle part of the story was not yet over.

The following Wednesday I was asked to teach at our Christian school chapel in Oldtown, Idaho, at the House of the Lord. I decided to share about my ministry in Japan and Indonesia. The photo that I had taken from the top floor of the Istiqlal Mosque was small. When I remembered that it was an important mosque, however, I thought to look through my library of books on Asia and Islam, thinking that just maybe I could find a photo of the mosque. In a large book called *Living Faith: Inside the Muslim World of Southeast Asia*, I discovered a two-page spread showing a photo of the inside of the Istiqlal Mosque looking down on the Muslim men praying. I was so excited to hold up the book to about eighty students in junior high and high school to show them what I had seen and to tell the story of how I had prayed for the salvation of these people. The students were surprised.[274]

After the chapel, one of our church leaders, Kathy Croston, came up to me and said, "Pastor Stan, can I see that photo again?" Afterward, she asked me to wait there and she went to her office. Soon she returned with a *National Geographic* magazine issue on the topic of Indonesia, with a picture in it of the inside of the Istiqlal Mosque. She then proceeded to tell me the following story: The week that I was in Japan, she taught children at our Thursday night service. Her desire was to impact them with the concept of missions, and her plan was to make them a little Japanese meal representing my trip to Japan. And she hoped to find something at our small community library about Indonesia.

---

274 Steve Raymer, *Living Faith: Inside the Muslim World of Southeast Asia* (Singapore: Asia Images Edition, 2001), 22_23.

The library had no books about Indonesia, but they did have *National Geographic* magazines available. She found one that featured Indonesia and—amazingly—it featured the photo taken from inside the Istiqlal Mosque, looking down on the worshipers at the exact same place where I had stood. At the Thursday night children's class, she showed them the picture and had them pray for me. They prayed that when I went to Indonesia the following week, somehow I would get to visit that very mosque and pray for those Muslims, that they would get saved. When she told me this, I was awestruck at the wonderful, miraculous God whom we serve, who could interconnect all of these events. Kathy told me that my little girls, Susanna and Liberty, were also in that class praying for me.

I learned from that experience that we should never underestimate the prayers of schoolteachers and children. Yet, the thing that struck me even deeper was that God cared for those Muslims who were there in that place. His desire was to see them come to know the truth and reality of the Lord Jesus Christ. I cannot prove it, but I believe that through the series of those prayer events, some of those Muslims were impacted to receive Christ.

VISIONS AND DREAMS

Each year many Christians and congregations join together to pray thirty days of prayer for Muslims around the world. Revelation 5:8 tells of "golden bowls full of incense, which are the prayers of the saints" (NKJV). The sweet aroma of our prayers may be part of why so many Muslims have been having dreams and visions about Jesus in the last few decades. I have met former Muslims in Pakistan who were drawn to our evangelistic-healing meetings because they had had dreams of Jesus and they wanted to find out more about Him. An ex-Muslim from Iran told me how he had an extensive dream about Jesus. He said that he had never really thought about Jesus, but all of a sudden, he was intrigued. As a scientist, he liked to investigate things. So, he began learning what he could about Jesus. He and his wife eventually gave their lives to Christ.

Taher was a dedicated Muslim in the Middle East. He was a respected Haji because he had made the pilgrimage to Mecca. His wife, too, had gone, but then she converted to Christianity. His daughter and son also converted. He got angry at them, quoted the Koran, beat them, and threatened to call the secret police. His family left him, fleeing to another country. When Tahir became lonely, he focused on Allah and the Koran. He said, "Please show me your face," but there was only silence. He began to question what he had believed all of his life and to wonder if perhaps his family was correct. He decided to pray. He prayed, "I will believe in the God who reveals Himself." Shortly after this, he had a dream of Jesus riding on a donkey and telling him that He would cleanse his sins. This dream occurred three times in a row. Taher woke up and immediately believed that Jesus was God. He then accepted Him as his Savior.[275]

In another supernatural encounter, one woman had a dream in which God told her that she would meet two women the next day and she was to do what they said. The next day she met two Christian women who led her to Jesus. In addition, a Shia seminary professor named Samir was mediating one day about rising above the clouds when suddenly he saw Jesus. In this vision, Jesus did not speak to him. Yet, over the next few days, he had four more encounters in which Jesus began to speak. This led to several times in which the Lord gave Samir assignments about reading certain passages of the Bible. Each time that Shamir saw Jesus, he was instructed to follow Him only. Eventually, Samir gave his life completely to Christ.[276] Also, a man had been training to become an imam in Ethiopia for twenty-four years. He studied in Saudi Arabia and returned with zeal to serve Allah in his own country. Then one night, he had an unexpected vision—a dream in which Jesus told him to read certain Koranic suras about Jesus and then to follow Him. In the next dream, he was told that he would be persecuted for following Jesus, but that he would be victorious. The imam's family and tribe did not like that he was beginning to follow Jesus, and he was accused of a crime that he did not commit and then sent to jail. However, in the court trial, he was found to be not guilty. He then helped more than two hundred other people to come to faith in Christ.[277]

275 Aimee Herd, "This Muslim Man Was Enraged with Christian Family Members until Jesus Visited Him Three Times in a Dream," *Open Doors USA* (May 12, 2014): breakingchristiannews.com.

276 Joel Rosenberg, Kindle Edition, Chapters 25, 29.

277 Janelle P., "After Dream of Jesus, Imam Renounces Islam," *Open Doors* (August

Today, there are numerous books, radio broadcasts, television shows, and Internet sites reporting that the number of visions and dreams that Muslims have been having about Jesus is on the rise. The phenomenon is gaining more and more recognition as individuals tell the stories of how visions of Jesus changed their lives. One source reports that in the last sixteen years, there have been well over a million dreams and visions of Jesus Christ documented in twenty-nine different countries. Who knows how many countless more have received such a miracle from God![278]

The prayers of Christians for others are a huge part of what is happening today. It is Spiritual Warfare 101. It is the "Air Force" of Christian warfare on behalf of a world of lost souls.

The prayer warrior S. D. Gordon simplified the concept of prayer this way:

> In its simplest meaning prayer has to do with conflict. Rightly understood it is the deciding factor in a spirit conflict. The scene of the conflict is the earth. The purpose of the conflict is to decide the control of the earth, and its inhabitants. The conflict runs back into the misty ages of the creation time. . . . Prayer is man giving God a footing on the contested territory of this earth. The man in full touch of purpose with God praying, insistently praying—that man is God's footing on the enemy's soil. The man wholly given over to God gives Him a new sub-headquarters on the battlefield from which to work out. And the Holy Spirit within that man, on the new spot, will insist on the enemy's retreat in Jesus the Victor's name. That is prayer. Shall we not, every one of us, increase God's footing down upon His prodigal earth![279]

As Christians, we are to pray for all men everywhere (1 Timothy 2:1–2). That includes our neighbors, communities, leaders, nation,

7, 2015): opendoorusa.org.
278 Michael Carr, "Rising Number of Muslims Reporting Dreams About Jesus," *WND* (November 1, 2014): wnd.com.
279 S. D. Gordon, *Quiet Talks on Prayer* (New York, NY: Grosset & Dunlap/Fleming H. Revell, 1941), 28, 35.

and the countries of our world. John Chrysostom (CE 350–407) wrote why, and his message is still valid for the Church today:

> The potency of prayer hath subdued the strength of fire; it hath bridled the rage of lions, hushed anarchy to rest, extinguished wars, appeased the elements, expelled demons, burst the chains of death, expanded the gates of heaven, assuaged diseases, repelled frauds, rescued cities from destruction, stayed the sun in its course, and arrested the progress of the thunderbolt.[280]

The Power of Love

The Christian Aid Mission released a story at the end of 2014 about tent churches springing up in the refugee camps of war-torn Syria and Iraq, because of the contrast with ISIS. The new converts to Christianity have been thoroughly amazed by the love of God.

> One reason they're [ISIS is] killing is that they wish to stop the rapid spread of Christianity. There has never been a time when a greater percentage of Syrian Muslims, in-country and refugees, have believed in Christ than in the past three years of civil war.
>
> "We all agree that it's the greatest awakening happening since the beginning of Islam," he said.
>
> The ministries also distribute food, medicine, and clothing, among other items—tangible evidence of the God of love. The Gospel message of love is the greatest evangelistic tool that Christian workers have, the director said, concurring that the love of Christ compared with the hatred of Muhammad in the Koran is shocking to Muslims.
>
> "When a Muslim reads about the unconditional love of Christ in the Gospel and how He forgave the adulteress, compared with the stoning of an adulteress by Muhammad, for example, the Muslim sees that God is not vengeful, but a loving God," one of the directors said.
>
> The first ministry leader added that the New Testament is about love, God giving Himself, and God wanting to be with people.

---

280 Chrysostom, as quoted in E. M. Bounds, *Purpose in Prayer* (New York, NY: Fleming H. Revell, 1920), 32.

"That's not something that makes sense in Islam," he said. "They're shocked that God can be that good. They say it cannot be that God is so loving, so caring. It's the love message that hits them the most."[281]

The Bible teaches us:

- "God is love" (1 John 4:16 NKJV).
- "We love Him because He first loved us" (1 John 4:19 NKJV).
- We are to speak "the truth in love" (Ephesians 4:15 NKJV).
- "For God so loved the world that He gave His only begotten Son" (John 3:16 NKJV).

God is the essence of love. The reason we are able even to know and express genuine love is because He loves us first. Many do not know of His love or accept the gift of His Son. Christians are to speak the truth to them in a spirit of charity.

Sometimes people misjudge or don't understand the love of Christians. Yet, that love has birthed many generations of missions, charity hospitals, food ministries, and prayer teams for Muslims and others. Love is the weapon in God's arsenal that disarms the toughest assailant and melts the hardest heart.

Here are some stories in which the love of God has changed Muslims. Shahrokh Afshar became a pastor at a Christian church for Iranians in Los Angeles. However, when he first came to the States, he argued his position with Christians. It was the love he saw in their lives that melted him. A Christian friend invited him to Thanksgiving dinner, and the simple prayer of a father saying grace touched him. From simple social gatherings to the Christians' warm acceptance, this brother gave his life to Christ. [282]

Fouad Masri, a Lebanese Christian in America, started the Crescent Project with the goal of helping Christians reach out to Muslims with compassion. Fouad says, "Our job is not to make a Muslim a Christian. Our job is to show them (Muslims) the love of Christ."

281 "Why Muslims Are Converting to Christ in the Face of ISIS Atrocities," *Christian Aid Mission* (December 4, 2014): christianaid.org.
282 "Escape from False Gods," *Charisma* (October 1997), 59.

Former Muslim and jihadist Dr. Tawfik Hamid was transformed by the love of Jesus. So now he wants to teach other Muslims about the love of Jesus Christ. He says, "The greatest problem in the Muslim world today is that they have no love in their hearts." The only way for any of us to really know love is to know the Lord Jesus Christ.[283]

Author Steve Sjogren wrote about love and deeds:

> Deeds of kindness get people's attention and often cause them to ask questions. Instead of having a forced presentation of the gospel to people who really aren't interested in what you have to say, we find people are curious and ask us to explain the message, which is vital to bringing someone to Christ without taking a sales approach. When we do speak, we must be sensitive to the level of receptivity of each person and explain the words of God's love in whatever way the hearer can understand. These words are the cognitive or conscious element of our evangelism. If we don't follow our actions with words, they will only know that we are nice people, not that God loves them.[284]

The Power of Witnessing

I personally do not think that it is easy to witness one-on-one to people, whether they are Muslims or not; it can be awkward to introduce the Gospel into a conversation, especially if it seems forced or is done in some type of methodological one-two-three, here-is-the-plan-for-salvation format. There are some people who have the gift of evangelism and they make it look easy, but I am not one of them. However, one thing I have noticed over the years in ministry as a pastor is that there appear to be seasons and times when individuals (or even groups) are more open to hear and accept the Gospel.

Yet, whether witnessing is easy or not, Christians *should* be witnesses in this world of the many wonderful things that Jesus has

---

283 Matthew Taylor, "Christian Compassion and the Muslim," *Focus on the Family* (March 2008): focusonthefamily.com.
284 Steve Sjogren, *Conspiracy of Kindness* (Ann Arbor, MI: Servant Publications, 1993), 22–23.

done, including His dying on the cross for our sins. For Christians who lack the self-confidence to witness about Jesus, there are a variety of courses that can be taken. These can be excellent to help equip Christians to share the most important elements of salvation in a persuasive method.

However, it is always important to remember that each Christian is a unique, special person in Christ (1 Peter 2:9–10) and that the Lord uses each one of us in a special way. So, really the first step for Christians to take when it comes to witnessing is to figure out what style of witnessing seems the most natural for them as an individual.

The New Testament reveals many different styles of witnessing. Here are some to consider. Christians may be able to relate to one or more of these approaches for their own lives.

i. Confrontational approach: Peter was bold, direct, and to the point.

ii. Intellectual approach: Paul was well educated. He could be confrontational, but he could also reason from Scripture. He could explain doctrine and give biblical proofs to reveal the nature of Jesus Christ.

iii. Testimonial approach: The blind man in John 9 didn't know a great deal about theology, but he could say, "One thing I know: that though I was blind, now I see" (verse 25, NKJV).

iv. Invitational approach: The Samaritan woman left her water jug at the well and invited her friends to come and hear a man "who told me all things that I ever did" (John 4:29 NKJV).

v. Interpersonal approach: Levi put on a banquet (Luke 5:29) for his tax-collecting friends in an effort to expose them to Jesus. (This is also known as friendship evangelism.)

vi. Service approach: Dorcas witnessed by serving others in Jesus' name, making clothes for the needy and poor (Acts 9:36).

vii. Writing approach: Luke was a doctor who knew how to share his faith through writing.

viii. Prayerful approach: Through prayer, God revealed to Peter a vision and an assignment to go witness to Cornelius (Acts 10).

ix. Encourager approach: Barnabas could win people over with his encouraging attitude (Acts 11:23–24).

x. Miraculous approach: Philip witnessed to people who were being healed (Acts 8:6–7).[285]

When it comes to witnessing to Muslims, the styles listed above can certainly help, but it is also important to get to know what things will move them to accept Christ. For example, J. D. Greear, a pastor and former missionary to Muslims, wrote an article entitled "A Gospel for the Muslim." In it, he says, "Muslims worldwide who come to faith in Christ consistently identify one of three factors leading to their conversion (or a combination of these three)."[286]

1. A copy of the Bible is placed in their hands.
2. They see the love in a Christian community.
3. They are visited with a supernatural dream or vision.

Being the recipient of a Christian's act of compassion and love can be a mighty witness. Receiving a vision or dream from Jesus can be a powerful witness. Yet, there is also the simple but great witness of the Bible. Sometimes the Word—all by itself—can lead people to the truth. Author William Miller tells of one such case:

> One day a shoemaker in Meshed brought home for his lunch some cheese which the grocer had wrapped in a page of the New Testament, which he was using for wrapping paper. After eating lunch Qasim picked up the piece of paper and read the story of the man who hired laborers for his vineyard, and at the end of day paid all the laborers the same wage, whether they had worked twelve hours or one. Qasim liked the story, and next day went again to the grocery

285 The first six are from Mark Mittleberg, "Discover Your Evangelism Style," *Discipleship Journal*, Issue 95 (September/October 1996). I came up with the last four.
286 J. D. Geear, *A Gospel for the Muslim* (2014): http://gcdiscipleship.com/a-gospel-for-the-muslim/ (accessed April 8, 2016).

> store and bought cheese, asking that it be wrapped in
> another page of that book. Finally, on the third day
> he bought what remained of the New Testament and
> showed it to his brother. The two of them then went
> to the missionary, who gave them a complete copy,
> and also gave them regular instruction in the Word of
> God. Both men were later baptized and were among
> the first believers in Meshed.[287]

Muslims seem to be searching for answers today in a world gone mad with wars, regime changes, ISIS, and refugees fleeing from homelands. Some who are searching find the answers in the Christian faith. Anecdotal evidence indicates that significant numbers of Muslim refugees who have fled to Europe are converting to Christianity. For instance, Trinity Church in the Berlin suburb of Steglitz has grown from 150 to 700 members in just two years. One in four confirmations at the Anglican Cathedral in Liverpool, UK, over the past year has been a convert from Islam.[288]

Today, technological advancements are making it possible for people all over the world to hear the Gospel message on the radio or see Christian evangelism messages on television. For example, 99 percent of the world's populations now have the opportunity to tune in to a Christian radio broadcast. There have been 4.1 billion viewings of the video entitled *Jesus*. For 2009, Campus Crusade for Christ reported that ten million Internet users came to faith in Christ through their Internet outreach branch alone. The New Testament has been translated into the languages of 94 percent of the world's population.[289]

Also, there are now free Bible apps for smartphones in numerous languages. A pastor whom I know in Lahore, Pakistan, takes a trip each year to the northern tribal areas to do evangelism. However,

---

287 William Miller, *A Christian Response to Islam* (Philipsburg, NJ: Presbyterian and Reformed Publishing Company, 1976), 113–114.

288 Harriet Sherwood and Philip Oltermann, "European Churches Say Growing Flock of Muslim Refugees Are Converting," *The Guardian* (June 5, 2016): theguardian.com.

289 "Statistics," *About Missions*, aboutmissions.org (accessed September 28, 2016).

he must be very careful. So, instead of just boldly proclaiming the Gospel message, he gives people phones with a Bible app on them. The audio Bible is then spoken to them in the Urdu language. This is an effective method. As they read and listen to the Bible, they want to know more and they reach out to him.

Father Zakaria Botros is a Coptic priest and a television evangelist in the Muslim world. He has received numerous death threats from fundamentalist Muslims because of his no-nonsense deconstruction of the Koran and his exposure of Muhammad's character issues. He is hated by millions in the Middle East, but they are also watching him. He gets millions of hits on his website, where he allows Muslims to ask their most difficult questions to online counselors, many of whom are former Muslims themselves. He challenges radical clerics to answer his refutations of the Koran. Botros figures that about one thousand Muslims per month pray to receive Christ through his programs.[290]

With Islam being the second-largest religion in the world, and, in one sense, the largest unreached group for evangelism, it would make sense that the largest majority of missionaries would be targeting Muslim nations. Unfortunately, the exact opposite is the truth. Of 140,000 Protestant missionaries, 74 percent work among nominal Christians—but only *6 percent* work among Muslims. Also, it is estimated that only .1 percent of all Christian giving is directed at missions efforts in the most unevangelized countries in the world.[291] These are in the 10/40 window. Pakistan is right in the midst of that window. The Punjab region of Pakistan, where Gate Breaker Ministries has started its Christian trade schools for women, GBM Hope Schools for slave children, and church plants, is considered by missiologists to be the most unreached place in the world per Christian worker.[292]

One important point to make about the proportion of Christian missionaries to Muslims is that some missionaries feel called

---

290 Joel C. Rosenberg, Kindle Edition, Chapter 27.
291 "Statistics," ibid.
292 Jason Mandryk, *Operation World: The Definitive Prayer Guide to Every Nation, Seventh Edition*, 664.

to a nation rather than to target a particular religious group. So, someone may feel inclined to minister in the Ukraine, and though that missionary may witness to people of many ethnic origins and religious backgrounds, this would also include the Tatar Muslims in that area.

There are specific mission agencies like Frontier Missions that specifically focus on Muslim populations. The missionaries who work with Frontier Missions have long-term strategies and thinking toward reaching the Muslim peoples. I have friends who are missionaries in the Middle East and Africa who are with Frontiers, and they form lasting relationships with the Muslim people in the regions where they live through their jobs and their neighborhoods. The light of Christ shines through them and eventually their work associates and neighbors begin asking them questions about Jesus. They do a great work.

Proverbs 11:30 tells us, "He who wins souls is wise" (NKJV). It is good to study the best ways to witness to Muslims. One of the things that has been discovered is that certain word choices when conveying the Gospel can produce a better understanding in Muslims. J. D. Greear noted the following:

> Three words describe the current Western approach to the gospel: *formula, forgiveness,* and *death.* We present the gospel as a *formula,* a series of propositions about God, which addresses our need for *forgiveness* from guilt, and which summarizes the means of attaining that forgiveness, the *death* of Jesus.
>
> While such a presentation accurately reflects aspects of the gospel, a more effective strategy among Muslims might focus on three "new words": **story, cleansing,** and **victory.**
>
> Instead of presenting the truth of the gospel propositionally as a formula, we ought simply to let the **story** of Scripture unfold. Muslims rarely come to faith in Christ through apologetic arguments and dogmatic proof-texting, but they often come to faith in Christ by studying the major stories of the Bible and encountering the gospel there.
>
> Instead of presenting the work of Christ in terms of forgive-

ness, we can emphasize the **cleansing** power of the gospel. Muslims understand the need for purification; they undergo a process of ritual cleansing, called *wudu*, every time they pray. Such a cleansing is only external, but Christ offers *wudu* for the soul.

Instead of presenting the death of Christ merely as a point of weakness, we should point to the **victory** inherent in Christ's work on the cross. Every time Muslims pray, they say that God is the "most powerful" and the "most merciful." Is not the cross the greatest demonstration of those two attributes? What greater demonstration of power is there than a God who overcame sin and death? God's greatness is actually shown in His humility. As Gregory of Nazianzus said, "The strength of a flame is shown by its ability to *burn downward*." And what greater demonstration of mercy is there than in Christ's death and resurrection? The God of the universe conquered sin and death in order to redeem us for Himself, through no merit of our own.[293]

There is no true salvation in Islam. A girl who stood in front of a Muslim judge in a Sharia court was asked, "Why did you leave Islam?"

"Because there is no salvation in Islam."

The judge turned to his advisers, experts in Islamic law, and asked them, "Is this true?" After consulting together, they answered that it was. The judge turned to the girl and said, "There is no case. You are free to go."[294]

While it would be inaccurate to say that all Muslims think Islam lacks salvation, the Muslim idea of salvation does not compare to the salvation offered by Christianity. Islamic salvation is based on works. The salvation of Christianity is based solely on the work of Christ at Calvary.

Christians should never underestimate the spiritual weapons of prayer, love, and witnessing. We were given the sword of His Word, so that Muslims all over the world can hear the good news of salvation in Jesus Christ.

---

293 J. D. Greear, ibid.
294 Copper, 293–294.

Finding the Peace of Christ

The historical worldview of Islam separated the world into two realms: *Dar-al-Islam* (House of Islam, or House of Peace) and *Dar-al-Harb* (House of War).[295] Islam condones war against everything outside of Islam. This has dominated Islam since its inception. There is no true peace in Islam.

Karim Shamsi-Basha had no real peace. Growing up as a Syrian Muslim, he feared Allah and felt like he had to work for his salvation. He was impacted by a Christian teenage friend who had peace and a relationship with God. He desired what his friend had, but he was stuck in fear and working to please Allah. Eventually, he moved to America to attend the University of Tennessee and then began a career in photography.

One day Karim had a brain aneurism that nearly cost him his life. A doctor was amazed that he survived. People told him that God had a reason for him to survive. This made him start searching for God in a deeper way. One day, he read the gospel of John in the New Testament. He read John 14:6, in which Jesus said, "I am the way, the truth, and the life. No one comes to the Father except through Me" (NKJV). This put him into a quandary, because he felt that he would be abandoning his Muslim family, who would not accept Christ. Then a friend told him that his first priority was between Karim and Jesus, and that God could take care of his family. So, Karim gave his life to Christ. He came to know a peace that passes understanding. Today, he loves Jesus and he knows that he is a son of the Father. He prays for his family to learn about the true peace that only Christ can offer.[296]

Though the world is full of fear, those who have come to know Jesus as Savior and Lord do not have to fear. The apostle Paul wrote about it to his disciple Timothy: "For God has not given us a spirit of fear, but of power and of love and of a sound mind" (2 Timothy 1:7

---

295 Armstrong, 30.

296 "Syrian Muslim Karim finds peace in Jesus and converts to Christianity," *The Light* (November 5, 2015): https://www.youtube.com/watch?v=2rlVapdBE-E. His book is: Karim Shamsi-Basha, *Paul and Me: A Journey to and from the Damascus Road, from Islam to Christ* (Birmingham, AL: Solid Ground Christian Books, 2013).

NKJV). God can give His people soundness of mind. Also, "God is not the author of confusion but of peace" (1 Corinthians 14:33 NKJV). Peace is important to God and was expressly emphasized by Jesus (Isa). On the night of the Last Supper, while warning the disciples that He would soon be betrayed, Jesus said,

> Peace I leave with you, My peace I give to you; not as the world gives do I give to you. Let not your heart be troubled, neither let it be afraid. . . . These things I have spoken to you, that in Me you may have peace. In the world you will have tribulation; but be of good cheer. I have overcome the world. (John 14:27; 16:33 NKJV)

Jesus wants to bring peace to His people, and according to Isaiah 9:6, Jesus is called the "Prince of Peace." He provides a mighty fortress against the principalities and powers of demonic forces. He offers true peace, even during times of intense stress.

After His resurrection, the apostle John tells us what Jesus said when He appeared alive to His disciples after the resurrection:

> The same day at evening, being the first day of the week, when the doors were shut where the disciples were assembled for fear of the Jews, Jesus came and stood in the midst, and said to them, "Peace be with you." (John 20:19 NKJV)

Jesus said, "Peace be with you." It is interesting to note that He spoke these words with the full knowledge that His disciples had previously abandoned Him in His hour of need, when Jesus was facing crucifixion. The Lord's openness to forgive and receive them should not have surprised the disciples. He had often done so.

Right now, the peace of Jesus is available for all who are willing to accept Him as Lord. During the Last Supper, Jesus prayed not only for those disciples who were present, but also for those who would believe in Him in the future.

> I do not pray for these alone, but also for those who will believe in Me through their word; that they all may be one, as You, Father, are in Me, and I in You; that they also may be one in Us,

that the world may believe that You sent Me. And the glory which You gave Me I have given them, that they may be one just as We are one: I in them, and You in Me; that they may be made perfect in one, and that the world may know that You have sent Me, and have loved them as You have loved Me. Father, I desire that they also whom You gave Me may be with Me where I am, that they may behold My glory which You have given Me; for You loved Me before the foundation of the world. O righteous Father! The world has not known You, but I have known You; and these have known that You sent Me. And I have declared to them Your name, and will declare it, that the love with which You loved Me may be in them, and I in them. (John 17:20–26 NKJV)

When you ask Jesus into your heart, He speaks peace into your life. He gives hope that calms your fears. He is the Master of peace, and He has opened the door for anyone to be close to Him. His words transform lives, heal hearts, and can change destiny.

Isaiah 53:5 tells us, "But he was wounded for our transgressions, He was bruised for our iniquities; the chastisement of our peace was upon Him, and by His stripes we are healed" (NKJV).

Colossians 3:15 says, "And let the peace of God rule in your hearts, to which also you were called in one body; and be thankful" (NKJV).

Second Thessalonians 3:16 states, "Now may the Lord of peace Himself give you peace always in every way. The Lord be with you all" (NKJV).

GLOSSARY

Abbasid Dynasty (CE 750–935). Dominating from Baghdad, it was known as the golden age of Islam.

Abdallah Ibn Jahsh. Team leader sent by Muhammad in the Nakha Raid.

'Abd al-Malik. Caliph who built the Dome of the Rock during CE 689–691.

'Abdulla bin Ubai bin Salul. Mistakenly accused Muhammad's wife, Aisha, of adultery and was executed.

Abraham. Father of Isaac and Ishmael. Muslims, Jews, and Christians view Abraham as a patriarch.

Abu Bakr. First caliph after Muhammad's death.

Ahzab. Third battle between Muhammad and the Meccans. Muhammad was victorious.

Aisha. Considered to be Muhammad's favorite wife.

Al-Aqsa Mosque. Located in Jerusalem.

Alawites. Minor sect of Islam that believes women do not have souls.

al-intifada. Arabic term for shaking off illegitimate political rule.

Ali. Fourth caliph and husband of Muhammad's daughter, Fatima. Shiites consider his descendants to be the true imams.

Allah. Islamic name for the God of Abraham. Original term probably referred to the moon deity and head of the Arabic pantheon of gods.

Al-Lat. Primary goddess daughter of Allah.

Al-Manat. Goddess daughter of Allah. Had scissors by which she cut the threads of human fate.

Al-Masih Isa. Arabic for "Jesus the Messiah."

Al-Qaeda. Islamic terrorist network started by Osama bin Laden.

Al-Rahman. Allah as the god of mercy and compassion.

Al-Uzza. Goddess daughter of Allah. Literally translated as "most powerful."

Anwar Sadat. Egyptian president who started peace talks with Israel in 1977, offered aid to the fledgling Afghani resistance in 1980, and was assassinated by Islamic fundamentalists in October 1981.

Arab. Any member of a Semitic people located in the southern Arabian Peninsula, or those from an Arabic-speaking group.

Ariel Sharon. Prime minister of Israel in 2001. Offered support to the U.S. after the September 11th attack.

Aus. Arab tribe that inhabited Medina during Muhammad's ascension to power.

ayas. Arabic term that means "signs" or "verses" in the Koran.

Badr. First battle between Muhammad and the Meccans.

Baha'u'llah. Nineteenth-century cofounder of Baha'ism, who claimed to be the return of the twelfth imam of Shiite tradition.

Caliph. "Rightly guided one," used to indicate a successor of Muhammad.

Dar-al-Harb. "House of war," referring to all territories outside of dar-al-Islam.

Dar-al-Islam. "House of Islam," or "house of peace."

Deen. Religious obligations as directed by the beliefs of Islam.

Dome of the Rock. Mosque built in Jerusalem in CE 691 to mark the spot where Muslims believe Muhammad began his night journey to heaven.

Eblis. Koranic name for Satan prior to his fall.

Egyptian Islamic Jihad. Egyptian fundamentalist groups responsible for terrorism.

Fahd. King of Saudi Arabia who drew criticism from Osama bin Laden and consequently revoked bin Laden's citizenship.

Faqih. Jurist or expert in Islamic law.

Fatrah. Intermission in Muhammad's writing of the Koran.

Fatwas. The religious decisions and decrees of Islam.

Fifth Column. Name for Islamic terrorist cells within the United States.

Fundamentalism. Form of religious extremism.

Gabriel. Intermediary angel that Islamic tradition says Allah used to reveal the Koran to Muhammad.

Hadith. Sacred collection of Islamic sayings and traditions.

Hagar. Mother of Ishmael.

Haj. A pilgrimage to Mecca; one of the five pillars of Islam.

Hanafites. Liberal school of Islamic law.

Hanbalites. Dogmatic school of Islamic law.

Hasan al-Banna. Founder of the Muslim Brotherhood in Egypt in 1928.

Hattin. Battle where Saladin defeated the Crusaders in 1187.

Hezbollah. Lebanese terrorist organization, translated the "Party of God."

Hosni Mubarak. Egyptian president who tried to rout Egyptian terrorist groups after the assassination of his predecessor, Anwar Sadat.

Imam. Religious leader of a mosque; also may refer to the "beliefs" of Islam.

Imamites. Name of the Twelver Shiite sect.

Injil. Arabic term for the gospels of the Bible.

Intifada. (Also *al-intifada*.) Specifies the clash between Palestinian Arabs and Israelis.

Isa. Arabic name for Jesus.

Ishmael. Son of Abraham who fathered the Bedouins and Arabs.

Ishmaelites. Name of the Sevener Shiite sect.

Islam. The religion founded by Muhammad. Literally means "submission."

Islamic revivalism. Politically correct term for Islamic fundamentalism.

Jafarites. Shiite school of Islamic law.

Jihad. "Struggle" or "effort"; the greater is a personal inner battle, while the lesser is an outer domestic battle to extend the dar-al-Islam into the dar-al-Harb.

Jinn. Genies or demons referred to in the Koran.

Kabah. Shrine in Mecca that stands as the center of Muslim worship.

Kainuka. Arabic tribe in Medina during Muhammad's ascension to power.

Khadijah. Muhammad's first wife.

Khomeini, Ayatollah. Religious revolutionary who overthrew the Shaw of Iran in 1979.

Koran. The holiest book of Islam. Literally means "recitation," referring to Muhammad's revelations from the angel Gabriel.

Malikites. Islamic school of law in Medina during Muhammad's reign.

Mauritania. African country in which slavery still exists under Islamic rule.

Mawalis. Literally "clients," referring to Islam converts.

Mecca. The holiest city of Islam; Muhammad's birthplace.

Medina. City where Muhammad came to power, waged his attacks against Mecca, and finally died.

Moghal Empire (CE 1526–1827). Located in India.

Mohammad Omar. Founded the Taliban in the mid-1990s and led the Afghani resistance against the United States in 2001.

Mossad. Israel's secret intelligence agency.

Mu'âwiya. First caliph of the Umayyad Dynasty.

Muhammad. Founder of Islam, author of the Koran, and considered in Islamic tradition as the greatest prophet of all times.

Muhammad al-Madhi. Twelfth and final imam of the Shiite movement; known as the "hidden imam."

Mujahadeen. Islamic warriors who formed the Afghani resistance against Russia in the 1980s; literally "those who wage the jihad."

Muslim. Believer of Islam; literally "one who is submitted" to Allah.

Muslim Brotherhood. Twentieth-century Egyptian fundamentalist group started by Hasan al-Banna.

Mu'tazilites. Group of ninth-century theologians who challenged the Koran as eternal and uncreated.

Nakha Raid. First raid that Muhammad authorized.

Nasser, Abdul. Egyptian ruler who in 1956 prompted the first of several wars with Israel.

Osama bin Laden. Leader and organizer of the Al-Qaeda terrorist network and primary suspect for numerous atrocities, including the World Trade Center attacks on September 11, 2001.

Ottoman Empire. Began in CE 1380 with vestiges of it lasting until after WWI.

Pahlevi, Muhammad Reza. Pro-Western Shaw of Iran ousted in 1979 by the Ayatollah Khomeini.

Palestinian Liberation Organization (PLO). Terrorist organization founded by Yassir Arafat to battle Israel in the intifada.

Pope Urban II. Proclaimed the need for the first crusade in CE 1095.

Qiblah. The direction that Muslims face during prayer.

Quraysh. Tribe in Mecca to which Muhammad belonged.

Rakahs. The traditional eight-step Islamic prayer that is repeated five times a day.

Ramadan. Islamic holy month set aside for fasting during sunlight hours.

Saddam Hussein. Former leader of Iraq who was responsible for the invasion of Kuwait in the early 1990s.

Safavid Empire (CE 1503–1722). Formed as a strong union between Turkish tribesmen and Persian bureaucratic leaders.

Saladin. Islamic leader who defeated the crusaders and recaptured Jerusalem in CE 1187.

Salat. Arabic term for "prayer."

Satanic verses. Controversial suras that were included in the Koran to permit worship of Allah's three goddess daughters. Considered by some to be led by a deception from Satan, especially when the verses were later changed.

Sawm. Term for the month of fasting during Ramadan.

Seljuk Turks (CE 990–1118). Turkish family that ruled and defeated the Byzantines at the Battle of Manizkurt in 1071.

Shahadah. The creed of Islam: "There is no god but Allah, and Muhammad is his messenger."

Shaitan. Arabic for "Satan."

Shafiites. The moderate school of Islamic law.

Sharia (or Shariah). The law of Islam; literally "the way."

Shiites. Radical Islamic sect that only recognizes the caliphs who have descended from Ali.

Shirk. Literally "blasphemy," as in associating other gods with Allah.

Sidrah-tree. The tree that is near God in paradise and beyond which no human and angel can pass.

Sudan. African country in which slavery still exists under Islamic rule.

Sunnah (sunna). Islamic customs.

Sunnites. Orthodox sect of Islam that includes the largest percentage of Muslims.

Sufi. The more animistic and mystical Islamic sect.

Sura. Chapters or portions of the Koran.

Tasbih (subhah). Islamic prayer breads.

Tawrat. The Torah—the first five books of the Old Testament.

Uhud. Muhammad's second battle with the Meccans.

Ulema (ulama). Scholars and guardians of the legal and religious traditions of Islam.

Umar. The second caliph to succeed Abu Bakr.

Umayyad Dynasty (CE 661–750). Replaced original caliphs and made Damascus the capital.

Ummah. The community of Muslim believers.

Umm al-kittab. The Koran as the preexistent tablet preserved in heaven.

'Umra. The smaller pilgrimage to Mecca, often in lieu of the haj.

Uthman. The third caliph who succeeded Umar.

Wahhabism. Extremist group founded by Muhammad ibn Abd al-Wahhab in the eighteenth century and linked to the House of Saud, from which came the present Saudi state.

Zabur. The Psalms.

Zaydites. Name of the Fiver Shiite sect of Islam.

Zakat. Literally "alms"; one of the five pillars of Islam.

BIBLIOGRAPHY

Adamson, Peter. *Philosophy in the Islamic World: A Very Short Introduction.* Oxford, England: Oxford University Press, 2015.

Alexander, Ruth. "Are there really 100,000 new martyrs each year?" *BBC News* (November 12, 2013): bbc.com.

Andrae, Tor. *Mohammad: The Man and His Faith,* 1936: reprint. Mineola, NY: Dover Publications, 2000.

Arabic Bible Outreach. www. Arabicbible.com. "Testimonial page."

Arlandson, James M. "Did Allah transform Jews into apes and pigs?" answering-islam.org.

Armstrong, Karen. *Islam: A Short History.* New York: Random House, 2000.

Asmarani, Devi. "Syariah law? Jakarta offers new criminal code instead." *Straight Times Indonesian Bureau,* October 19, 2001.

"Attack on Christian church killed 16." MSNBC. October 29, 2001, www.nbc.com.

Ayoub, Mahmoud M. "Toward an Islamic Christology: The Death of Jesus: Reality or Delusion." *Muslim World,* 1980.

Backgrounder—Terrorism. www.Nsi.org/Library/Terrorism/facterr.html.

Barna, George. "Statistics." www.barna.org.

Bayat, Mojdeh., and Mohammad Ali Jamnia. *Tales from the Land of the Sufis.* Boston, MA: Shambhala Publications, 2001.

Belz, Mindy. "We Are the World." *World Magazine,* September 22, 2001.

Blair, David. "Friday prayers in the Islamic Republic of Iran—but where are the worshippers?" *The Telegraph* (August 1, 2015): telegraph.co.uk.

Bodansky, Yossef. *Bin Laden: The Man Who Declared War on America.* Roseville, CA: Prima Publishing/Random House, 2001.

Booker, Richard. *Blow the Trumpet in Zion.* Shippensburg, PA: Destiny Image Publishers, 1992.

Bounds, E. M. *Purpose in Prayer.* New York, NY: Fleming H. Revell Company, 1920.

Braswell, George W. Jr. *Islam: Its Prophets, Peoples, Politics and Power.* Nashville, TN: Broadman & Holman Publishers, 1996.

Berggren, Vanja. "Female Genital Mutilation: Studies on primary and repeat female genital cutting." Thesis, Department of Public Health Sciences Division of International Health (IHCAR) Karolinska Institute, Stockholm, Sweden, 2005.

Burton, Dan. "Preparing for the War on Terrorism." Washington, D.C: Committee on Government Reform, September 20, 2001.

Carlson, Ron. Christian Ministries International. personal e-mail. Eden Prairie, MN. 2001.

_____, and Ed Decker. *Fast Facts on False Religions*. Eugene, OR: Harvest House Publishers, 1994.

Carr, Michael. "Rising Number of Muslims Reporting Dreams About Jesus." *WND* (November 1, 2014): wnd.com.

CBS. *60 Minutes*. 25 November 2001.

_____. "Cheers to Jeers in Kuwait." *60 Minutes*. November 18, 2001. http://www.cbsnews.com/60-minutes/

"Christianity 2015: Religious Diversity and Personal Contact." *International Bulletin on Missionary Research*, Vol. 39, No 1 (January 2015) 29.

"Christian Persecution." *Open Doors*. No date. opendoorsusa.org,

Chronology of Terror. www.cnn.com, September 12, 2001.

Churchill, Winston. *The River War*, First Edition, Vol. II,. London: Longmans, Green & Co., 1899.

Clarke, Adam. *Adam Clarke's Commentary on the Holy Bible*. Grand Rapids, MI: Baker Book House, 1987.

Classe, Cyril. *The Concise Encyclopedia of Islam*. London: Stacey International, 1989.

Clement, "First Epistle of Clement", chapter 7, *Ante-Nicene Fathers: Volume 9*. Peabody, MA: Hendrickson Publishers, Inc., 2004.

Cloud, John. "What Is Al-Qaeda Without Its Boss?" *Time*, November 26, 2001.

Cooper, Anne. *Ishmael My Brother: A Christian Introduction to Islam*. Crowborough, East Sussex, Great Britain: MARC, 1997.

Daughenbaugh, Wes. *The Heart God Hears*. Chelalis, WA: Gospel Net Ministries, 1996.

Dawson, Christopher. *Religion and the Rise of Western Culture,* Image Books edition. New York: Doubleday, 1991.

Durie, Mark. "Salafis and the Muslim Brotherhood: What is the difference?" *Middle East Forum* (June 6, 2013): meforum.org.

"Education and Scientific Development in the OIC member countries." *Statistical, Economic and Social Research and Training Centre for Islamic Countries*, SESRIC, 2013.

Eerdman's Handbook to the History of Christianity. Grand Rapids, MI: Wm. B. Eerdman's Publishing Company, 1977.

Elliot, Michael. "Hate Club." *Time*. November 12, 2001.

Ellis, Mark. "Islamic Terrorist Hunted a Pastor Until Jesus Gave Him an Unusual Vision." *Charisma News* (April 21, 2016): charismanews.com.

"Escape from False Gods." *Charisma* (October, 1997): 59.

Esposito, John L. *Islamic Threat: Myth or Reality?* third edition. New York: Oxford University Press, 1999.

Esther, Gulshan. *The Torn Veil*. Fort Washington, PA: Christian Literature Crusade, 1998.

Faber, Lindsay. "A Zionist in Andalusia's golden age." *U.S. News & World Report* 127 (August 16–23, 1999): No. 750.

Farrel, Elisabeth. "Escape from False Gods." *Charisma*, October 1997.

Fazal, Rizwan, Pastor and Director of GBM Hope Schools in Pakistan. Interview by author. Lahore, Pakistan, October 21, 2016.

Fleming, S. F. *Gate Breakers: Answering Cults and World Religions with Prayer, Love and Witnessing.* Seattle, WA: Selah Publishing, 1998.

Flinchbaugh , C. Hope. "Christian Workers from United States Remain Jailed in Afghanistan." *Charisma,* December 2001.

Foxe, John. *Foxe's Book of Martyrs.* Springfield, PA: Whitaker House, 1981.

Gabriel, Mark A. *Islam and Terrorism: Revised and Updated Edition.* Lake Mary, FL: Charisma Media/Charisma House Book Group, 2015.

Gordon, S. D. *Quiet Talks on Prayer.* New York, NY: Grosset & Dunlap/Fleming H. Revell, 1941.

Geear, J. D. *A Gospel for the Muslim* (2014): http://gcdiscipleship.com/a-gospel-for-the-muslim/.

Greenberger, Robert S., and Alix Freedman. "Sergeant served U.S. and bin Laden." MSNBC, November 11, 2001.

Guillaume, Alfred. *Islam.* London: Penguin Books, 1954.

Hadith. Volume 1, Numbers 211, 345, date unknown.

Hag, Noor ul. *The Mercy of Allah.* Minneapolis, MN: Center for Ministry to Muslims, 1996.

Hinnells, John R. *A Handbook of Living Religions.* New York, NY: Penguin Books. 1987.

Jenkins, Philip. *The Next Christendom: The Coming of Global Christianity, Third Edition.* New York: Oxford University Press, 2011.

Jones, Bob. "Morning of Terrors." *World Magazine,* September 18, 2001.

Josephus, Flavius. *The Complete Works of Josephus.* Translated by William Whiston. Grand Rapids, MI: Kregel Publications, 1980.

Halverson, Dean. *The Compact Guide to World Religions.* Minneapolis, MN: Bethany House Publishers, 1996.

Harden, Donald. *The Phoenicians: Ancient Peoples and Places.* New York, NY: Frederick A. Praeger, Publisher, 1963.

Herd, Aimee. "This Muslim Man Was Enraged with Christian Family Members until Jesus Visited Him Three Times in a Dream." *Open Doors USA* (May 12, 2014): breakingchristiannews.com.

Herrington, Carson. *Arts of the Islamic World: A Teacher's Guide* (Washington D.C.: Smithsonian Institution, 2002), 6.

Hiebert, Paul G. and Frances F. *Case Studies in Missions.* Grand Rapids, MI: Baker Book House, 1987.

Hurgronji. *Mohammedanism.* Westport, CT: Hyperion Press, 1981.

"Israel Fires Missiles Near Arafat Headquarters." MSNBC. December 3, 2001. www.nbc.com.

"Islamic Terror on American Soil." *The Religion of Peace.* thereligionofpeace.com.

"Jihadism: Tracking a month of deadly attacks." BBC News (December 11, 2014): bbc.com.

Jones, Nelson. "Are Christians really the world's most persecuted religious group?" *New Statesman* (April 10, 2014): newstatesman.com.

Kaplan, David E., and Kevin Whitelaw. "The CEO of Terror, Inc." *U.S. News & World Report.* October 1, 2001.

Kelsay, John. *Islam and War: A Study in Comparative Ethics.* Louisville, KY: Westminster/John Knox Press, 1993.

Kettler, Sara. "Malala Yousafzai Biography." http://www.biography.com/people/malala-yousafzai-21362253#after-the-attack biography.com.

Khomeini. *Islam and Revolution: Writings and Declarations.* London: KRI, 1981.

Kierkegaard, Soren. *Fear and Trembling* (London, England: Penguin Books, 2006), 18.

Koran. Translated by J. M. Rodwell. London. Orion Publishing Group. Rutland, Vermont. Charles E. Tuttle Co., 1994.

Korkut, Dede, M.D. *Life Alert: The Medical Case of Muhammad.* Enumclaw, WA: Winepress Publishing, 2001.

Küng, Hans. *Christianity and the World Religions: Paths to Dialogue with Islam, Hinduism, and Buddhism.* London: Collins, 1986.

LaCasse, Alexander, "How many Muslim extremists are there? Just the facts, please." Christian Science Monitor (January 13, 2015).

Landay, Jonathan, and Warren Strobel, and Phil Stewart. "Islamic State ruling aims to settle who can have sex with female slaves." *CNN* (December 29, 2015): truthandgrace.com.

Lewis, Bernard. *Islam in History: Ideas, People, and Events in the Middle East.* Chicago, IL: Open Court, 1993.

_____. "Jihad vs. Crusade." *The Wall Street Journal,* September 27, 2001.

_____. *Peace Encyclopedia,* quoted in Mitchell Bard, "The Pro-Islam Jews," *Judaism* (Fall, 1968): 401.

Light the Window Video. Virginia Beach, VA: CBN International, 1995.

"List of Islamic Terror: 2014." *The Religion of Peace.* thereligionofpeace.com.

Lynch, Justin. "Women Are Sex Slaves in South Sudan's Civil War." *The Daily Beast* (March 13, 2016): the dailybeast.com.

McClintock, John, and James Strong. *Cyclopedia of Biblical Theological, and Ecclesiastical Literature.* Baker Book House, 1981.

Maalouf, Amin. *The Crusades Through Arab Eyes.* New York: Schocken Books, 1984.

Madden, Thomas F. *A Concise History of the Crusades.* Oxford, England: Rowman & Littlefield Publishers, Inc., 1999.

_____. "The Real History of the Crusades." *Crisis Magazine* (April 1 2002).

Mandyrk, Jason. *Operation World: The Definitive Prayer Guide to Every Nation, Seventh Edition.* Colorado Springs, CO: Biblica Publishing, 2010.

Maqsood, Ruqaiyyah. *Teach Yourself Islam.* Lincolnwood, IL: NTC/Contemporary Publishing, 1994.

Martyr, Justin. *The Apology,* lxvii, quoted in Henry Bettenson, *The Early Christian Fathers.* Oxford: Oxford University Press, 1969.

Mass, Warren. "Congress Releases Classified '28 Pages' of 9/11 Commission Report," *The New American* (July 18, 2016): thenewamerican.com.

Mather, George A., and Larry A. Nichols. *Dictionary of Cults, Sects, Religions and the Occult*. Grand Rapids, MI: Zondervan Publishing House, 1993.

Mazhar, Uzma. "Rape, Zina, or Incest: Islamic Perspective." Muslim Access (2002): webcitation.org.

McGlinchey, Brian. "Saudi Government Links to 9/11 Shouldn't Stay Secret," *28 Pages* (June 12, 2016): 28pages.org.

Melhem, Hisham. "The Barbarians within our Gates." *Politico Magazine* (September 18, 2014): www.politico.com/magazine/story/2014/09/the-barbarians-within-our-gates-111116.

Melito, "Discourse of the Cross." *Ante-Nicene Fathers: Volume 8, 4th Edition*. Peabody, MA: Hendrickson Publishers, 2004.

Meo, Nick. "Half a million African slaves are at the heart of Mauritania's presidential election." (July 12, 2009): webcitation.org.

Merriam-Webster Thesaurus. Springfield, MA: Merriam-Webster, Inc., 1989.

Mikkelson, Barbara and David P. "False Prophecy." www.snopes.com.

Miller, William. *A Christian Response to Islam*. Phillipsburg, NJ: Presbyterian and Reformed Publishing Company, 1976.

"Ministry Redeems More Than 2,000 Slaves." *Maranatha Christian Journal*, July 11, 1999, www.Mcjonline.com/news/news3228.htm.

Minor, David. "Strongholds." (Oldtown, ID) Taped message at House of the Lord. 14 January 1996.

Mirza, Aliya. "2,000 minorities' girls converted to Islam forcibly: report." *Daily Times* (September 5, 2012): webcitation.org, and Muslim Statistics/Slavery at wikiislam.net.Mittleberg, Mark. "Discover Your Evangelism Style." *Discipleship Journal*, Issue 95 (September/October 1996).

Mohaddessin, Mohammad. *Islamic Fundamentalism: The New Global Threat*. Washington, DC: Seven Locks Press, 1993.

Mordecai, Victor. *Is Fanatic Islam A Global Threat?* Jerusalem, 1997.

Morey, Robert. *The Islamic Invasion: Confronting the World's Fastest Growing Religion*. Eugene, OR: Harvest House Publishers, 1992.

Morin, Harry. *Responding to Muslims*. Springfield, MO: Center for Ministry to Muslims, 2000.

Muehlenberg, Bill. *Culture Watch*, quoted on belief.net.com. No date.

Muir, William. *The Life of Mahomet*, Volume 4 (1861).

Muir, William, Rede Lecture delivered at Cambridge in 1881: Asia. 2nd ed., revised and corrected. Published 1909 by E. Stanford in London.

Musk, Bill A. *Passionate Believing*. Tunbridge Wells: Monarch Publications, 1992.

"Muslim Publics Share Concerns about Extremist Groups." *PEW Research Center* (September 10, 2013): www.pewglobal.org.

Mustafa, Nadia. "After 50 Years, a Muslim Split." *Time*. November 5, 2001.

Neill, Stephen. *Crisis in Belief*. London: Hodder and Stoughton, 1984.

Olasky, Marvin. "Islamic worldview and how it differs from Christianity." *World Magazine*, October 27, 2001.

Oxford Dictionary of World Religions.(Oxford: Oxford University Press, 1997.

P., Janelle. "After Dream of Jesus, Imam Renounces Islam," *Open Doors* (August 7, 2015): opendoorusa.org.

Parkinson, Tony. "'Bin Laden' voices new threat to Australia." *The Age* (November 14, 2002): theage.com.au.

Parrinder, Geoffrey. *Jesus in the Qur'an.* New York, NY: Oxford University Press, 1977.

Parshall, Phil. *The Cross and the Crescent.* Wheaton, IL: Tyndale House Publishers, 1989.

Pascal, Blaise. *Thoughts on Religion and Philosophy.* W. Collins, 1838.

Pement, Eric. "Louis Farrakhan and the Nation of Islam." *Christian Research Institute* (June 9, 2009): equip.org; "Nation of Islam," ibid.

"Praying through the Window IV: Light the Window." *AD 2000 & Beyond.* "Statistics." www.Ad2000.org/.Adherents.com/rel_USA.html#religions.

"Profile of Osama bin Laden." Anti-Defamation League. www.adl.org/terrorism_America/bin_l.asp.

Qur'an. Translated by M. A. S. Abdel Haleem. Oxford, England: Oxford University Press, 2010.

Random House Webster's College Dictionary. New York: Random House, 1992.

Rashid, Ahmed. *Militant Islam, Oil, & Fundamentalism in Central Asia.* New Haven: Yale University Press, 2001.

Raymer, Steve. *Living Faith: Inside the Muslim World of Southeast Asia.* Singapore: Asia Images Edition, 2001.

Redeker, Robert. "*Face aux intimidations islamistes, que doit faire le monde libre?*" Le Figaro (September 2006).

Reid, Tim. "'Islam is violent,' says President Obama's new pastor Carey Cash." *The Times* (October 15, 2009): as recorded in "Quotations on Islam from Notable Non-Muslims." wikiislam.net.

Renard, John. *Seven Doors to Islam: Spirituality and the Religious Life of Muslims.* Berkeley, CA: University of California Press, 1996.

Ridenour, Fritz. *So What's the Difference?* Ventura, CA: Regal Books, 2001.

Rippin, Andrew, and Jan Knappert. *Textual Sources for the Study of Islam.* Chicago: University of Chicago Press, 1990.

Rosenburg, Joel C. *Inside the Revolution.* Carol Stream, IL: Tyndale House Publishers, 2011, Kindle Edition.

Rumph, Jane. *Stories from the Front Lines: Power Evangelism in Today's World.* Grand Rapids: MI: Chosen Books, 1996.

Runciman, Steven. *The First Crusade*—Canto Edition. New York: Cambridge University Press. 1992. _____. *A History of the Crusades: Volume III, The Kingdom of Acre and the Later Crusades.* New York: Cambridge University Press, 1999.

_____. *The Fall of Constantinople, 1453.* New York: Cambridge University Press, 2001.

Rushdie, Salman. "Islam: I don't like the word Islamophobia." October 2, 2012: webcitian.org.

Saleeb, Abdul. "Answering Misha 'al Al-Kadhi's question about Jesus." January 20, 1985: answering-islam.org.

Schimmel, Annemarie, and Abdoljavad Falaturi. *We Believe in One God.* New York, NY: The Seabury Press, 1979.

Segal, Ronald. *Islam's Black Slaves.* New York, NY: Farrar, Straus, and Giroux, 2001.

Sell, Canon. *Studies in Islam.* London: Diocesan Press, 1928.

"75% of new U.S. Muslim converts leave within three years." *Muslim Statistics.* December 14, 2012: muslimstatistics.wordpress.com.

Shapiro, Ben. "The Myth of the Tiny Radical Muslim Minority." *Breitbart.* September 4, 2014. breitbart.com.

Servier, Andre. *L'islam et la psychologie du musulman.* London: Chapman Hall LTD, 1924.

Shamoun, Sam. "The Quran, Allah and Plurality Issues." No date. Answering-islam.org.

Shamsi-Basha, Karim. *Paul and Me: A Journey to and from the Damascus Road, from Islam to Christ.* Birmingham, AL: Solid Ground Christian Books, 2013.

Sherwood, Harriet, and Philip Oltermann. "European Churches say growing flock of Muslim refugees are converting." *The Guardian.* June 5, 2016: theguardian.com.

Shibley, David. *A Force in the Earth: The Charismatic Renewal and World Evangelism.* Altamonte Springs, FL: Creation House, 1990.

Silvoso, Ed. *That None Should Perish: How to Reach Entire Cities for Christ through Prayer Evangelism.* Ventura, CA: Regal Books, 1994.

Sjogren, Steve. *Conspiracy of Kindness.* Ann Arbor, MI: Servant Publications, 1993.

"Slavery in Sudan." *Christian Solidarity International.* No date. csi-usa.org.

Smith, Wendell. *God Can Still Bless America.* Kirkland, WA: Publication of the City Church, 2001.

Sperry, Paul. "How US covered up Saudi role in 9/11." *New York Post.* April 17, 2016. nypost.com.

Stott, John R. W. "God on the Gallows." *Christianity Today.* January 27, 1987.

Strong, James. *The New Strong's Exhaustive Concordance of the Bible.* Nashville, TN: Thomas Nelson Publishers, 1995.

Swerdlow, Joel L. "Alexandria, Cordoba, and New York: A Tale of Three Cities." *National Geographic.* August 1999: 196, No. 2.

Taylor, Jeff. "I Must Get a Bible." *Charisma*, October 1997, 14.Taylor, Matthew. "Christian Compassion and the Muslim." *Focus on the Family.* March, 2008. focusonthefamily.com.

Tertullian. Adversus Marcionem ii. 27, quoted in Henry Bettenson, *The Early Church Fathers.* Oxford: Oxford University Press, 1969.

"The Future of World Religions: Population Growth Projections, 2010–2050." Pew Research Center. April 2, 2015: pewforum.org.

"The Reconquest." *Si, Spain*. May 1994: www.sispain.org/english/hist ory/reconque.html.

"The Relativities and the Rhetoric." CNN's Special Report. October 2001. "The Truth About Islam and Female Circumcision." *Inside Islam: Dialogues and Debates*. February 18, 2011: insideislam.wisc.edu.

"The world's five most dangerous countries for women: A Thomson Reuters Foundation global poll of experts." June 15, 2011: webcitation.org.

"The World's Muslims: Unity and Diversity." Chapter Two. *Pew Research Center*. August 9, 2012: pewforum.org.

Tyrangiel, Josh. "Did You Hear About?" *Time*. October 8, 2001.

Us-israel.org. "Relationship between U.S. and Israel."

_____. "Timeline."

_____. Selection from *The Los Angeles Times*. 20 September 2001.

Vahanian, Gabriel. *Wait without Idols*. New York: George Braziller, 1964.

Vallely, Paul. "The vicious schism between Sunni and Shia has been poisoning Islam for 1,400 years—and it is getting worse." *The Independent*. February 19, 2014: www.independent.co.uk/.

Van De Mieroop, Marc. *The Ancient Mesopotamian City*. Oxford, England: Oxford University Press, 1999.

Viorst, Milton. *In the Shadow of the Prophet: The Struggle for the Soul of Islam*. New York: Anchor Books/Doubleday, 1998.

Vu, Michelle A. "Interview: Ex Muslim Women on Life under Sharia Law." *Christian Post*, April 9, 2009: christianpost.com.

Wagner, Clarence H., Jr. "Between a Rock and a Holy Site." *Christianity Today*. February 5, 2001.

"Walid's Testimony." *Answering Islam*. No date. http://answering-islam.org/Testimonies/walid.html.

Walker, James K. *Index of Cults and Religions*. The Watchman Expositor. Birmingham, AL: Watchman Fellowship, 2000.

Warren, Lindy. "German Evangelist Takes Gospel to Pakistan." *Charisma,* December 2001.

Watt, William Montgomery. *Muslim—Christian Encounters: Perceptions and Misperceptions*. New York: Routledge, 1991.

Weiss, Walter M. *Islam: An Illustrated Historical Overview*. Hauppauge, NY: Barron's Educational Series, 2000.

Welch, William M. "Christian hostages beheaded in Islamic State video." *USA Today*. February 16, 2015: usatoday.com.

Welsh, Teresa. "Study: Christians are the most persecuted religious group in the world." *McClatchy DC*. June 27, 2016: mcclatchydc.com.

"Why Muslims Are Converting to Christ in the Face of ISIS Atrocities." *Christian Aid Mission*. December 4, 2014: christianaid.org.

Window Watchman II. Colorado Springs, CO: Christian Information Network, 1997.

Woodberry, J. Dudley. *Muslims & Christians on the Emmaus Road.* Monrovia, CA: MARC Publications, 1989.

Zunz, Olivier, and Alan S. Kahan. "Alexis de Tocqueville." *The Toqueville Reader.* Blackwell Publishing, 2002: 229.

To order additional copies of:

Allah Weeps:
A Christian Perspective of Modern Radical Islam

Large orders contact:
Selah Publishing Group
Toll free in the U.S.
1 (800) 917-2665
www.selahbooks.com

Individual orders visit:
www.amazon.com

Also available in Kindle e-book format

CPSIA information can be obtained
at www.ICGtesting.com
Printed in the USA
LVOW03s1503160517
534667LV00033B/1713/P